In this new book, Terry Sanderson reveals how gay people can achieve a more balanced, happy and fulfilled life by using proven assertiveness techniques.

Gay people are indoctrinated from an early age with the idea that their sexuality is sad, bad or hilarious. In adult life, these negative feelings can lead to many problems, ranging from isolation to suicidal impulses.

This book will help gay men understand the origin of this uneasiness with their sexuality, and how it can be turned into positive action for change. Assertively Gay is packed with practical information and useful tips.

ASSERTIVELY GAY

How To Build Gay Self-Esteem

Terry Sanderson

The Other Way Press

First published in Great Britain, 1993 by :

The Other Way Press
P O Box 130 London W5 1DQ
Tel: 081 - 998 1519

© **Terry Sanderson, 1993**

British Library Cataloguing in Publication data is available
for this book from the British Library.

ISBN 0 948982 04 7

Distributed by: Turnaround Distribution
27 Horsell Road, London   N5 1XL
Tel: 071 - 609 7836

Printed by: Bailes Fastprint, Houghton-le-Spring, DH5 8AN
Tel: 091 - 584 6097

Also by Terry Sanderson:

How To Be a Happy Homosexual

The Potts Correspondence and Other Gay Humour

Making Gay Relationships Work

A Stranger in the Family: how to cope if your child is gay

ASSERTIVELY GAY

Terry Sanderson is a journalist and frequent contributor to the gay press. His *Mediawatch* column has been running for many years in *Gay Times* and has a large and enthusiastic following. Less well-known is his long counselling experience both within the gay community and, for several years, on the problem page at *Woman's Own*.

His other books include the best-selling *How to be a Happy Homosexual; Making Gay Relationships Work; A Stranger in the Family - how to cope if your child is gay;* and a collection of humorous essays, *The Potts Correspondence*. He has lived for the past eleven years in London with his lover, Keith.

《《 》》

Dedicated to Keith,

whom I love and cherish.

Contents

Introduction 1

1. How Gay Self-Esteem is Damaged ... 6

2. Choices 30

3. Introducing Assertiveness 70

4. Assertiveness Techniques 90

5. Assertiveness and Coming Out 123

6. Gaining Confidence 144

7. The Loneliness Trap...................... 159

8. Relationships 180

9. Assertiveness and Sex 201

10. Moving On 227

INTRODUCTION

It has been said - by Alfred Kinsey among others - that the word "homosexual" should be used only as an adjective describing a sexual act, and not as a noun defining a person. To Kinsey, who was the father of sex research, there was no such thing as "a homosexual", only homosexual acts. Conversely, there could be no such thing as "a heterosexual" either. So, he argued, given that all people are capable of performing homosexual or heterosexual acts, we should really just think of ourselves as *sexual* people rather than homo- or hetero-.

All this gives rise to the argument that in labelling ourselves "homosexual" we have created a rod for our own back, but even Kinsey admitted that there are some people - a large minority in fact - whose sexual preferences are entirely or overwhelmingly homosexual. These people, who have little or no interest in relating sexually to the opposite sex, have to find some way of defining their feelings, and this is where the concept of being "gay" came from. We needed to identify and give a name to our sexual preference so that we could make sense of our feelings. We needed to construct lives that were meaningful in a world that insisted that they had no meaning. The label which we have invented represents more than just sexual acts, it represents a lifestyle. And so, defining ourselves as "gay people" is not the same as calling ourselves "homosexuals". A gay person has made a commitment to a particular way of living and of feeling.

There are some men whose orientation is mostly heterosexually directed, but who have occasional homosexual impulses, and who seek out male partners to satisfy that urge.

Assertively Gay

These men would not wish to label themselves "gay", because their main preference is directed at the opposite sex - they, by default, have been labelled "straight" (or, more contentiously, "normal"). It shouldn't automatically be assumed, therefore, that because someone occasionally seeks out a same-sex partner they are simply closeted gay people.

Sexuality is fluid. If we apply the label gay or straight to ourselves, then it is a conscious decision. We do it on the basis of what we feel. But we do not have to swear an affidavit or register our preference with the Government. If our feelings change, then they change, and there would be nothing to stop us changing the label.

The famous Kinsey sex research carried out between 1948 and 1963 showed that roughly one in three men and one in five women have had at least some overt homosexual experience between their teens and middle age. For many of them that experience had been more than incidental. Nearly 21% of white, college-educated men and 7% of white, college-educated women report having had sex with two or more persons of their own gender and/or having homosexual sex six or more times. Percentages for non-college educated men and women are 28% and 5% respectively. Black people reported fewer incidences of homosexual experience - only 16% of black college educated men and 3% of women.

This research enabled the Kinsey Institute to produce a scale - a continuum of sexual behaviour - which runs from zero to six, to indicate the degree of homosexuality or heterosexuality that an individual has in his or her personality. Zero indicates that a person is entirely heterosexually-oriented, and has never had a homosexual experience, while six indicates that a person is completely homosexually oriented and has had no heterosexual experience. In between, where most people are situated, there is a mixture of "largely homosexual, but with incidental heterosexual history" (5 on the scale); "largely homosexual with a distinct heterosexual history" (4); "equally heterosexual and homosexual" (3); "largely heterosexual with a distinct homosexual history" (2) and so on. It is clear from this that a large number of people who aren't gay will indulge an occasional urge, or satisfy their curiosity about homosexuality.

This was illustrated, too, in another large-scale survey of male sexuality, carried out by the American author Shere Hite in the 1970s. Part of her questionnaire asked straight-identified men what they felt about homosexual sex, and whether they would like to try it. 18% of her respondents who considered themselves to be straight said they would like to try fellatio with another man. To the question "Do you like, or would you like, to be rectally penetrated?" 16% of men who identified themselves as straight said they had been, or would like to be, penetrated by a penis.

In the anecdotes which were solicited from the straight men who responded to the questionnaire, it became apparent that having gay sex is a fairly common fantasy among heterosexual men. Few, however, were willing to allow their curiosity to stray beyond fantasy, such is the strength of the social taboos against homosexual sex.

Those men who are mainly heterosexual, but who *are* experimenting with gay sex should not be confused with those men whose overwhelming preference is homosexual, but who are pretending that it is otherwise. These men, whose orientation is largely or wholly homosexual, seek to avoid the label "gay" because it carries with it a stigma. By "passing for straight" they imagine that they will not have to suffer the "consequences" of being gay. That may be true, but there will be other, probably much more severe, consequences in the long term.

Those people who define themselves as bisexual - capable of relating to both sexes - have accepted that their sexuality is not fixed, although most would admit that they have a greater preference in one direction or the other.

Our critics will say that by applying the label "gay" to ourselves, we have limited our options. The underlying message is that we have deliberately opted to forego the "privilege" of being straight in an overwhelmingly heterosexual society. You will often hear straight people maintaining that their way of life is "natural", "normal", "right and proper" and so forth; they are utterly convinced of its superiority. Even straight people who consider themselves to be liberal-minded will display this sexual chauvinism. A friend told of an occasion when he 'came out' to a heterosexual relative; the woman had said: "It makes no difference. I don't care what your sexuality is, I still love you." She was fond of him and when he moved to London to find a more satisfying life than the one he had lived so far in the small Welsh village where he had been brought up, she kept in touch and followed his fortunes. A little while later he had told her that he was moving into a flat-share with three other gay men. "Are you sure you're doing the right thing?" asked the woman. "Won't that make your life a little bit *too* gay?"

Would she have asked the same question if he had not mentioned the sexuality of his flatmates? Or would she simply have assumed that they were straight, and so thought no more about it?

We cannot deny that heterosexual people in society today have advantages that are denied to gay people. For instance, heterosexuals can be parents much more easily than we can (but in the light of modern technology and science, that can be overcome) and they have legal rights and concessions that are not available to gay people (but in a more just society that,

4

too, can be changed). Equality is not an impossible dream but, if we're realistic, its achievement must be seen as a long-term goal. All the same, it is perfectly possible for gay and straight people to accept each other and coexist peacefully and it is already happening all over the country.

So let us be clear at whom this book is aimed: it is for those men who know that their true identity is a gay one and who want more than anything to relate to other men in a loving and sexual way. Or, as the writer Christopher Isherwood put it: "The real clue to your sex-orientation lies in your romantic feelings rather than your sexual feelings. If you are really gay, you are able to fall in love with him, not just enjoy having sex with him."

For the rest of this book, the terms "homosexual men" and "gay men" will refer interchangeably to those of us who have chosen that definition as the truest description of our sexuality.

1: HOW GAY SELF-ESTEEM IS DAMAGED

What Is Self-Esteem?

We all know vaguely what is meant by self-esteem, but what are the practical consequences of having *low* self-esteem? How does it affect our day to day functioning? In this book we're going to look particularly at *gay* self-esteem, the way we regard our sexuality, and how easily - or uneasily - it sits with other aspects of our lives.

As usual, we begin with the Oxford English Dictionary, which defines esteem as: "to think of favourably or to regard highly". It follows from this that *self*-esteem means to think of yourself favourably and regard yourself highly. This is not the same as being conceited ("having too high an opinion of one's own beauty, ability, etc." - OED). Thinking favourably of yourself means that you like yourself - all parts of yourself - and are convinced that you have value.

However, it isn't quite as easy as that. Our sense of worth can vary in different areas of our life. Often we can present a confident, competent version of ourselves in certain situations, while at other times we might appear diffident, nervous and completely lost. Some people are extremely good at their jobs and are much admired in their field. These same individuals may behave quite differently at home with their partner or family - the self-reliant worker might suddenly become a cringing and manipulated creature, totally controlled by guilt. Some people are excellent bosses, but terrible subordinates; others are fine with their peers, but have problems with authority figures.

For gay people, the biggest problems are likely to arise in those areas of life involving their sexuality - we have, after all been raised to despise our sexuality. We have been brought up to consider it mad, sad, bad or hilarious. None of us have escaped this indoctrination. Nobody told us during our all-important formative years, that it would be OK to have strong, loving feelings towards a member of our own sex; the probability is that we received the opposite message. Our parents, if they mentioned the topic at all, probably told us to "watch out for people like that". Our school friends and youthful contemporaries might have reserved their most derisive insults for "poofs" and "queers". Every time we open a newspaper there seems to be some critical or insulting article. I doubt if there is a single gay person in the world whose self-esteem has not been harmed to some extent by this relentless prejudice.

The Effects Of Social Referencing

Psychologists are pretty much agreed that what happens to us in the first five years of our life can profoundly influence what kind of adult we will turn out to be. If we are raised to feel good about ourselves, if our parents encourage us and nurture our sense of worth, then we will probably be fine in most areas of life. But, in those decisive years, it is almost certain that we will either hear nothing at all about homosexuality or that we will pick up negative messages. Perhaps our parents discouraged us from playing with "inappropriate" toys or ridiculed any interest we might have shown in "feminine" pursuits. The sense of what is "right and what is "wrong" for boys and what is "right" and "wrong" for girls is pervasive in our culture even in these supposedly enlightened times. From the cradle, when boys are dressed in blue and girls in pink, right through school, when peer pressure insists that boys are rough and girls are gentle, the message is being instilled. Men have a particular role and so do women and there is little scope for cross-over.

Children don't even need to be directly told that they should hate homosexuals, they can pick up the hostility and revulsion simply by studying their parents' reactions. Some parents have a conscience about influencing their children with their own prejudices and try very hard not to do so. A mother who has an irrational fear of the dark or spiders or thunder, but who does not wish to communicate this fear to her child, might attempt to cover up her dread when in the presence of the frightening object. But the child will be able to pick up the suppressed emotion from the subtlest of clues - a pursed mouth, a tense hand or an involuntary shudder. This is called *social referencing*, and has been defined by the psychologists Campos and Sternberg as: "the tendency of a person of any age to seek out emotional information from another person, and to use that information to make sense of an event that is otherwise ambiguous or beyond the person's own intrinsic appraisal capabilities."

Social referencing takes place most often in infancy; the child looks to an object or situation, and then to the parent to see what the appropriate reaction should be - is it safe, is it friendly or is it to be avoided? Depending on the facial expression or body language of the parent, the child will know how to react to this unfamiliar object or situation in future.

The same goes for social prejudice. If, for instance, parents see a programme about homosexuals on television, they might avoid making any direct comment about the

8

programme, but they might hasten to change the channel, or simply leave the room because they don't want to see it. The child will pick up this uncomfortable reaction, whatever efforts the parents make to conceal it, and they will assimilate the prejudice into themselves. If that child, who has internalised and accepted his parents' homophobia, should then go on to find that he himself is gay, there is an immediate conflict. The idea that one boy might find another boy sexually attractive is derided almost universally, and although boys might well experiment sexually with each other, this is usually not considered by most of them to be "homosexuality", but simply a method of satisfying an urgent new sexual curiosity.

Gay people are surrounded by hostility and negative messages about who they are. Although there are more positive images than ever before, these are still few and far between and often kept away from the people who need to see them most. Section 28 of the Local Government Act crushed attempts in the 1980s to introduce into schools a more sympathetic view of homosexuals in Britain. The opinion that children must be protected from the "corrupting influences" of homosexuality still holds sway. Once more the assumption is that *all* children are heterosexual, and that none of them need reassurance about their sexuality. And so another generation of homosexuals is silently tortured, and their self-esteem is battered in a thousand different ways. Tabloid newspapers heap insult and humiliation upon us, television comedies continue to make "jokes" about gay people which rest on damaging stereotypes. It is still acceptable to make comments about limp wrists and sexual "abnormality". Children who are going to grow up gay are surrounded by this aggression and hatred. They internalise it. Many come to loathe themselves.

Persistent Urges

Most gay people hide their true selves for most of those formative years in a psychological closet that shields them from the hatred. From the beginning they are given the 'benefit of the doubt', assumed to be heterosexual. We do not discourage this false assumption in our loved ones, because it is easier, safer and more convenient to pass for straight. Nobody wants to be rejected by their significant others, especially when feeling isolated and vulnerable, harbouring feelings we have come to regard as unacceptable.

Yet, however unwelcome the homosexual urges might be, they refuse to go away. The more we deny them, the more pressing they seem to become. At some stage most of us have an overwhelming urge to do something about those feelings. We want to love in the way that we know is right for us.

As we mature, some of us feel that we cannot sustain the pretence any longer and we come out of the closet. We take the risk of upsetting those who are close to us, we gamble with the relationships that have so far been central to our lives - with our parents, our brothers and sisters, friends and work colleagues. We tell them that we are gay, and we hope that they will at least try to understand and accept. Most of the time they do their best. They do not want to lose us any more than we want to lose them. Sometimes, because of their homophobic feelings, they just cannot cope and they reject us or we reject them. We might lose people from our lives, but we have done what we felt was necessary in order to live honestly, openly and - we hope - happily.

That, though, is only the first step in a long, long journey. Those lonely years when we were in the closet, trying to sort out what we wanted from life and trying to gain the courage to come out, will have damaged us more profoundly than we realise. They may have left us with a residue of self-loathing so deep that we may have been driven to seeking psychiatric help or even to attempt suicide.

What Negative Conditioning Can Do

No-one should underestimate the power of this early negative conditioning. You don't have to look far within the gay community to see the harm that has been done to individuals by these years of systematic oppression and self-oppression. Many people who function healthily and well in other areas of life may become disturbed and unhappy when they try to explore their sexuality. This damaged sexual self-esteem can manifest itself in many ways; Gordon Allport, in his book *The Nature of Prejudice* (Addison-Wesley, 1954) wrote: "Every form of ego defence may be found among members of every persecuted group. Some will handle their minority group membership easily, with surprisingly little evidence in their personality that this membership is of any concern to them. Others will show a mixture of desirable and undesirable compensations. Some will be so rebellious that they will develop many ugly defences."

Gordon Allport identified eleven negative ways in which some people respond to being part of a stigmatised group. Many of these will be familiar to gay people who are struggling with internalised homophobia and self-loathing. If you are still unsure about the value of your sexuality, ask yourself if any of these features apply to you:

1. Denial. An individual who feels deeply unhappy about his gay feelings may deny to others, and even to himself, that he is gay or has any kind of sexual feelings towards members of his own sex. This constant denial simply reinforces in this individual's mind that his sexuality is undesirable and unacceptable.

In a recent biography of the writer Daphne du Maurier, it was revealed that while she was writing "yearning love letters" to another woman and having a passionate physical affair with Gertrude Lawrence, she wrote: "By God and by Christ if anyone should call that sort of love by that unattractive word that begins with 'L', I'd tear their guts out."

2. **An obsessive concern about being "found out"**. The closeted gay person will become deeply anxious about possible exposure and this worry will lead him into being defensive, suspicious and insecure. The prospect of his homosexuality being disclosed becomes, in his mind, the most fearful thing that could possibly happen. That fear can rapidly snowball into a life-controlling obsession which requires a tissue of lies and fabrications to keep it under control.

3. **Social withdrawal and passivity**. Many gay people feel that it safer to withdraw as much as possible from socialising and therefore reduce the risk of exposure, rejection and humiliation. If they avoid people who might expose or persecute them, then their anxiety level reduces, but their isolation and loneliness increases. Passivity, too, indicates a desire not to "rock the boat". If you're always at other people's beck and call, always friendly and obliging, it is less likely that they will challenge you on the basis of your sexuality, but it also means that you will be open to exploitation.

4. **Clowning.** Being the court jester is a common defence mechanism used by some gay people in order to deflect criticism and gain approval from those whom they fear. It can

be a useful survival strategy in some cases, but if it becomes the prevailing characteristic, it can limit opportunities and prevent the person being taken seriously.

5. Slyness and cunning. Often it is necessary in order to survive to become sharper and more indirect in our dealings with other people. We may need to become artful liars in order to avoid disapproval or prejudice. This can lead to a massive loss of self-esteem, and can seriously interfere with our relationships with other people.

6. Identification with the dominant group. When gay people "take sides" with homophobic heterosexuals it is a sure sign that they don't like themselves very much. For instance, if a straight person says: "Homosexuals should keep quiet and stop flaunting it. I don't want to see two men holding hands in the street, it's embarrassing and makes me feel sick" and you find yourself agreeing with them, then you are colluding with the homophobia expressed in the remark. You are, in effect, denying your own right to an equal place in society. Gay people who are identifying with the dominant group will often trot out the arguments proposed by tabloid newspapers such as "Children need to be protected" or "Gay people are all dreadfully promiscuous".

7. Aggression against and criticism of one's own group. There are many homosexuals who are ferocious critics of their gay brothers. Many of them are closeted people who are trying to deflect attention from their own sexuality by loudly and publicly disapproving of other people's. This phenomenon was identified by Laud Humphries, in his book *Tearoom Trade*, and labelled 'the breastplate of righteousness'. This protective breastplate is assumed by those self-hating gay men who think that they will gain prestige among heterosexuals by being vociferously anti-gay. There have been several notorious examples of this effect when viciously homophobic people in public life have subsequently turned out to be gay themselves. Perhaps the most famous was J. Edgar Hoover, the man who ran the FBI in America for more than forty-eight years. Hoover was homosexual and had a long relationship with his (male) personal assistant, but he made a point of ostentatiously persecuting other gay people. His purges of 'faggots' (his word) from the State Department and armed forces, wrecked the careers and lives of thousands of lesbians and gay men.

The breastplate of righteousness is the product of deeply internalised homophobic feelings.

8. **Directing prejudice and discrimination against other minorities**. There seems to be a need within most human beings to feel superior to someone else, and not to be bottom of the heap or last in the pecking order. This creates problems within minority groups. For example, many black people hate homosexuals, many Christians hate Jews and many homosexuals are racist.

9. **Excessive neuroticism.** Some gay people with deep insecurities about their sexuality become neurotic and unstable. This manifests itself in many ways, but there is little doubt that some of us can become either too passive, very aggressive or unapproachable in some other way. We cease to be able to function healthily, and in many instances we may need psychiatric help. So profound is our anxiety about our sexuality, that it pushes us into neuroses.

10.**Internalising and acting out negative social definitions and stereotypes.** We may have internalised, and accepted as true, ideas of what homosexuals are: sexually aggressive or compulsive, seeking out degrading or dangerous sexual pastimes, inveterate liars, can't be trusted with children, invariably effeminate and weak. If we have no positive role model to contradict these damaging definitions, we might feel compelled to live up to them.

11.**Excessive striving for status to compensate for feelings of inferiority.** We mentioned earlier that some gay people excel in their career, gaining wide admiration and prestige for their commitment and dedication. But this commitment comes at the expense of other aspects of life - love and relationships - and might be seen as an avoidance of these. But the need to be seen as "better than the rest" can become an obsession with some gay people, completely dominating their life. They are compensating for the anxiety and feelings of inferiority that comes from loathing their gayness.

None of these behaviours are intrinsic to gay people - that is to say, we do not behave in such negative and destructive ways *because* we are homosexual; the behaviours are simply defence mechanisms against discrimination and persecution. There's no doubt, though, that when people adopt such responses they reinforce within themselves the negative stereotypes and beliefs that hold them back from their full potential.

What Self Hatred Can Do

A vivid illustration of where a damaged sense of sexual self-esteem can lead was given in a Channel Four TV programme, broadcast in early 1992, which investigated the activities of the so-called "ex-gay" movement.

The "ex-gay" movement is run by Christian fundamentalists and claims to be able to "cure" homosexuals through a process of "counselling" and prayer. There are a growing number of organisations that undertake this work ("Pilot", "Exodus", "The True Freedom Trust" and "L.I.F.E." are just four names to watch out for).

One individual at the forefront of the "sexual healing" fraternity is George Harvey. Mr Harvey has for years been running an organisation that claims to help homosexuals who are unhappy with their orientation to "give up their sin" and become heterosexual. He has achieved this transformation in some cases, he says, within seven weeks. Mr Harvey took up his "ministry to heal homosexuals" when his own gay son, Simon, committed suicide. Poor Simon had been severely damaged by the disapproval that he felt all around him. He was deeply afraid of hurting his father and considered that the only way out of his dilemma was to take his own life. The TV programme included extracts from Simon's farewell letter to his parents: "Dear Mum and Dad," he wrote "By the time you receive this I will be dead. I cannot begin to describe the depths I have been through trying to marry being gay with being a Christian. I knew I could no longer control my sexual urges and I desperately needed someone to love. I finally found someone who loved me. It probably disgusts you that a man could love a man."

Mr Harvey says that he blames himself for his son's death. He proposes that a faulty relationship during childhood "robbed Simon of his masculinity". He does not make clear what he means by this statement, but it appears to demonstrate a profound ignorance of the nature of homosexuality. However, there can be little doubt that Mr Harvey's brand of Christianity, which takes everything that is written in the Bible literally, will have had a hand in crushing Simon's sense of sexual self-worth. Although Simon had found a lover, it is unlikely that the relationship would have succeeded under such heavy internal and external pressures.

Also on the programme was Michael Bussee, a founder of Exodus International, an umbrella organisation for all these "sexual healing" ministries. Mr Bussee admits that although he has "counselled" literally hundreds of gay men, not one of them has truly changed their sexual orientation. "Some of them have become celibate and some got involved in marriages where they had no sexual attraction to their wives," he said.

He recalled one man who, despite a genuine desire to change, was tormented that all the counselling and prayer was having no effect upon his feelings. "He felt so bad," says Mr Bussee, "that he took a straight edged razor and repeatedly slashed his genitals, and then poured Draino on the wounds. I remember he came in the next day and I said, Michael, why did you do that? and he said, because I'm not changing and I feel terrible. And I said, how do you feel after you did that? And he said, better."

This case is a further illustration of how far a damaged sense of sexual self-esteem can push people, and it is not an isolated incident. The ex-gay movement in the USA makes the dubious claim that it has "counselled" and "cured" 100,000 homosexual people.

The indoctrination sessions are, in the main, run by people who are "ex-gay" themselves, and claim to have not only given up homosexuality but actually to have become heterosexual. Testimony on the TV programme from people who had volunteered for the counselling indicated that often the counsellors themselves were far from "cured" and used the session as a means of expressing their barely suppressed sexuality. Several men told of the "holy hugs" that are part of the proceedings, and which in many cases turned out to be less than innocent.

Assertively Gay

What is it that has caused these people to hate their sexuality so much that they go to such lengths to try and change it? How have they reached the conclusion that not only are their own homosexual feelings loathsome, but so are those of other people? The explanation, they say, is that their sexual feelings are at odds with biblical teaching; the real explanation is often that their sense of self-worth has been deeply distorted by a lifetime of negative indoctrination. They have been systematically taught to hate themselves. Naturally if someone comes along proclaiming a "cure", such self-hating gay people will jump at the opportunity. They become willing victims in their own exploitation. Their deep unhappiness is exploited by misguided individuals some of whom use religion as a cover for their own desperate homophobia.

Another example of this inability to accept sexuality was given in an article in *The Guardian* newspaper (21 March, 1992) which concerned men who join religious orders. The author, Peter Stanford, wrote: "Throughout history one powerful attraction of the seminaries has been that - on the surface at least - they are sanitised sex-free zones and therefore attractive to those who don't want to deal with their sexuality. In the recent past, the church has encouraged gay men finding it hard to come to terms with their sexuality to consider becoming priests." The article includes an interview with an ex-seminarian named James who tells how "a vocation to the priesthood" turned out to be an explicit denial of his sexuality. He says: "I saw a vocation as a way of defeating my homosexuality and being comfortable with Christ. I felt as if the black hole into which I was falling was in check. It was as if I was too weak to survive in the world...If you took a random group of ten seminarians four of them would probably say they were gay...If I was cynical I would judge these vocations as avoidance."

We may not all be as deeply scarred as those who approach the ex-gay movement (or dubious psychoanalysts who also promise "cures"), but most of us have been touched in some way by this internalised homophobia. We have absorbed and accepted the opinions that are all around us, and we have done it at a time in our lives when we were susceptible, alone and insecure. We learned many things when we were children: that fire burns, that roads are dangerous, that mother feeds us when we are hungry - and that homosexuality is not acceptable.

The restrictions against homosexuality have always been severe. Once it was usual for those who were discovered in compromising homosexual situations to be imprisoned and socially ostracised in much the same way as were serious criminals. Let us not forget that it is barely a hundred years ago that Oscar Wilde was serving a prison sentence *with hard labour* because he was homosexual.

Those cruel laws are changing, if only slowly. The social taboo, however, is not so easily challenged and homosexuality is still regarded as an unacceptable alternative by most people. Every generation is saturated - either directly or indirectly - with the same message: being straight is great, but being gay is far from okay. For most young gay people, the first inkling that they have a homosexual orientation will be frightening and unwelcome. The internal battle that is going on between the knowledge of one's own feelings and the desire not to have them, can, as we have seen, cause people to behave in ways which are nothing short of disastrous for their lives, resulting in problems with alcoholism, drug abuse, depression, sexual irresponsibility and shattered relationships.

Accentuate The Positive

There are degrees of adjustment, though. Not all gay people feel that they need to adopt destructive strategies in order to survive, and slowly a new and more confident generation is emerging. But that confidence is not gained easily, it comes only after years of painful struggle involving many setbacks and self-betrayals. The good news is that we *can* progress. After all, everyone was born with high self-esteem. Little children are not burdened with fears about their worth, they take it for granted that they are the centre of their own universe. It is only little by little that the demolition job is carried out on our self-esteem. But what has been knocked down can be built again. We can repair our damaged gay self-esteem and move forward into a happier life if we make the choice to do so. If we are stuck in one of the traps described above, we can escape from it. To do that we have to break patterns of habitual negative thinking about ourselves. We have to challenge thoughts that we have taken for granted as being accurate. It will be necessary to separate the facts about our sexuality from the mythology with which we have indoctrinated. That isn't easy.

If we go back to the book by Gordon Allport which was mentioned earlier, and from which the eleven negative behaviours were extracted, we can find that there are also positive responses that can be adopted by people who are members of a stigmatised minority. These, as far as gay people are concerned, only come when some effort has been made to accommodate homosexuality into the rest of one's personality, when a process which has been termed "stigma conversion" has occurred. Laud Humphries, in another book *Out of the Closets: The Sociology of Homosexual Liberation* (Prentice-Hall, 1972), described this process as follows: "In converting his stigma, the oppressed person emerges from a stigmatised cocoon as a transformed creature, one characterised by the spreading of political wings. At some point in the process, the politicised 'deviant' gains a new identity, an heroic self-image as crusader in a political cause." You may not want to be a political crusader, but there is no doubt that if you are going to make an effort to live a gay life, you are making a political decision.

The first sign of a recovering sense of gay self-esteem would be when you began to feel more sympathetic to and "connected" with other gay people. You would be able to feel outrage and sorrow when fellow homosexuals are discriminated against. You would begin to understand the nature of prejudice and how it works; this will bring you to sympathise with the problems of other minorities, too. You will begin to feel that the battle is well worth the fighting, and you will consciously strive to improve your lot in life. You will come to see homophobia as an obstacle to be surmounted and not as a prison from which there is no escape. You will begin to feel that you can fight back when you feel your homosexuality is being used against you, and you may even wish to become involved in the wider struggle for gay rights.

The damage that has been done - and continues to be done - to gay people is scandalous, but now we are beginning to speak out for ourselves and demand that this degrading treatment stops. We want to spare future generations the unhappy early years that most of us have had to endure.

I hope that readers of this book who want to escape, who want to have a life that is meaningful to them, will be able to work on those areas of their lives in which their sexuality creates problems. The aim is to rescue our sexuality from the limbo to which some of us have consigned it and re integrate it as an influential part of our personality. Once it has assumed its proper place, it can rapidly be brought into proportion. We can stop worrying about it, and start living.

An Invaluable Tool

Assertiveness is one of the most successful psychological techniques to change negative patterns of behaviour. Thousands of people have found that by learning about and practising assertiveness, they have begun to function much more effectively. As a "life-skill", assertiveness has many general applications, but in this book we will apply it specifically to the areas of life that cause difficulties for gay people. By learning to cope with difficult situations in ways that lead us to succeed, we increase our confidence. The more we succeed, the greater becomes our self-esteem. With persistence, assertiveness can become second nature and helps us bring our life under control. It can help us realise that the destructive and limiting mechanisms we use to avoid conflict or change can be challenged and overcome. We will have genuine confidence, rather than the ersatz variety that was sung about in the famous tune "Whenever I feel afraid I whistle a happy tune". We are going to try and move on from the stage of covering up our sexuality by whistling a happy, but dishonest, tune. We are going to stop avoiding and lying about our sexuality and eventually we will reach the point where we genuinely accept its value and influence.

Hopefully by learning to deal with the situations that frighten us (like coming out, or being found out, for instance) we will be able to enjoy our homosexuality for its great potential, and not regard it as a source of dread and loathing.

What Is Assertiveness?

Although assertiveness is a popular subject for workshops, seminars and training courses, it is widely misunderstood and some people still find it difficult to grasp the essential difference between assertiveness and aggressiveness. You can be sure, for instance, that if you announce at work that you are going on an assertiveness course someone will immediately start making jokes about it being a waste of time: "You're bossy and big-headed enough already", they'll quip. Of course, they've missed the point. Being bad-tempered, loud-mouthed, manipulative or hostile is not being assertive.

Many assertiveness courses are aimed specifically at women. It is assumed that because of women's traditionally inferior position in society, they have a special need to be taught the principles and techniques of assertiveness. In order to survive in a world which seems to be run by power-hungry men, they need to be able to insist that they are heard. That's true, of course, but now the question has to be put - what's the relevance for gay men? Where and how can assertiveness help us achieve our goal of raising our sexual self-esteem?

The answer is that gay men, like women, have been regarded as inferior over the centuries. We have been "kept in our place" by the dominant heterosexual culture which demands that we stay hidden and silent - or else risk the wrath of the 'respectable' majority. Only a few short decades ago there were cruel, but effective, ways of keeping us subdued: public humiliation and ostracism were the best we could hope for; jail, violent hatred, physical abuse or murder were the worst. Pretty good incentives, I'm sure you'll agree, to keep a low profile.

Much of that has changed. We are no longer completely illegal, some of our lovemaking - in some circumstances and beyond a certain age - is tolerated and 'permitted' by law. Public attitudes, too, are slowly changing and there is no longer a need to regard the damage that is done to us in our childhood to be irreparable. Society has now granted us enough space to be able to heal ourselves - but we're expected to do it ourselves, no help will be provided from community resources.

There are similarities here with the changing role of women. Once it was automatically assumed that women would take second place, would refrain - except in freakish circumstances - from trying to occupy centre stage in public life. So strong were the cultural restraints that many women accepted that this was their lot in life - just as many gay people assumed that it was *their* lot to be fugitives from society and outcasts from themselves. Before the mid-sixties it very rarely occurred to women that they could be independently successful and that their talents could compete directly with men, just as it rarely occurred to homosexuals that they could have a place in society on their own terms.

I was watching an old 1950s episode of *I Love Lucy* recently. It reflected the attitude of its time perfectly. Lucy was the archetypal housewife of that period, staying at home to look after the baby while famous husband Ricky Ricardo went out to earn a living doing an interesting job. It was Lucy's role to clean the apartment, feed the baby, squabble with the neighbours, get her hair done and imagine that the most wonderful thing in the world would be if her husband bought her a fur coat. She was totally dependent on Ricky for her financial security. If she wanted a hat, she had to supplicate herself at the altar of Ricky's ego to get it. If she wanted a holiday, she had to beg for it.

In real life, of course, Lucille Ball was one of the most successful businesswomen in American history. But she was an example of the freakishness I referred to above. And to illustrate how slowly things are changing, we should bear in mind that in Britain, even in the 90s, only two per cent of business executives are female and they earn an average of £10,000 less per year than their male counterparts.

Nowadays more and more women are demanding equality. They are pushing themselves into jobs which had previously been denied them, they are refusing to accept that men have the first option on the best things in life. And so it is with the gay community. At long last we seem to have found a voice. More and more of us are coming out and saying: "I'm going to live life on my own terms and not to pretend to be something I'm not." Just as women want to have available all the options that men have, then so do gay people want to have all the options that heterosexuals have. The fly in the ointment is that, after centuries of oppression and repression, both women and gay men are having trouble with their self-esteem.

There are flaws in the analogy of course. Gay men are, after all, *men.* If they can pass for straight they can enjoy all the privileges that other men enjoy - with the exception of an honest love life. If they can't - or won't - pass for straight, there may be barriers put in their way: sometimes obvious, sometimes more subtle and difficult to challenge.

These subtle, and not so subtle, pressures to keep quiet can gradually erode gay people's belief in themselves as whole human beings. Then begins a destructive process of self-separation. Many gay men lead what they consider to be their conventional or "real" life openly and with pride, while their emotional life is relegated to secrecy or even complete denial. This process of separating and distancing ourselves from aspects of our personality was described by psychologist Nathaniel Branden in his book *The Disowned Self* (Bantam Books, 1972). He wrote: "Man is an organism - a living entity - who is conscious; which is to say, he is a person. And he can relate to the world effectively only as a person, only as an integrated unity. One of the greatest acts of self-delusion is for an individual to imagine that he can preserve the clarity of his thinking after he has become disconnected from his own person, from the reality of his emotional experience...When a person denies his real needs, the inevitable outcome is the creation of an unreal self - the personality he presents to the world."

Tragically, Dr Brandon's description applies to countless gay people who have denied and put aside their feelings. It is unhealthy to continue this disconnection, and great efforts must be made to face up to the truth and work through the pain that will allow you to integrate your sexuality back into your own life.

Here are stories from a few gay people, who consider themselves to be well-adjusted in most respects, talking about situations that leave them frightened and anxious:

> *"The prospect of telling my parents that I'm gay makes me feel quite nauseous. I have a good gay life, with a man I adore, but it's lived well away from my parents, and they don't know a thing about it. I've thought about coming out to them, but when I visualise the scene, I turn to jelly and put it out of my mind. I have become distanced from my family, whereas before I used to be very close to them. But only by keeping them away can I be sure that they won't find out."*

> "I'd love to have a boyfriend of my own, a regular lover who I could live with and have a deep relationship with, but I'm absolutely hopeless at meeting people. I'm convinced that no-one could possibly want to spend the rest of their lives with me - not when there are so many other really attractive people to choose from."

"I'm effeminate - I'm quite well aware of that - people have been telling me since I was a child. At school I was called a sissy and a pansy and made fun of. Even my parents thought I was laughable. Wherever I've gone there is always somebody who wants to take the mickey. I've tried to change, but it's just the way I am. I'm very self-conscious when I speak to strangers, and worry all the time what they think about me."

"We live in a council flat on an estate that is a bit rough. When the neighbours discovered that we were two gay men living together, the trouble started. Kids would stand outside the door chanting, and there was graffiti all over the walls. We felt threatened every time we went out, and had no idea what to do for the best. Sometimes I shout things back at them, but they just laugh and then I feel even worse than before. Because we are so isolated here, I'm beginning to think there is something wrong with us."

"I have great problems saying 'no' to people. Like the other day, I met this fabulous man in the local pub and went home with him. I thought it was a dream come true, but then he started wanting to have unsafe sex. I didn't like to say anything to him about it being dangerous, in case he got annoyed. I even had a packet of condoms in my pocket, but I daren't get them out in case he was offended by the suggestion that he might have Aids, so I went along with it. I wish I hadn't now, and I'm petrified. I'd made a pact with myself not to have unsafe sex with

anyone, but I don't really know how to tell people without upsetting them."

"Although I'm out at work, I don't make a big thing about my gayness, but there is one particular woman who is making my life a misery. She makes remarks in front of other people - things like 'There's some queer folk knocking about these days' and she's always reading out loud from the papers about 'poofs' and 'dykes'. I just don't know what to say, and I tend to shrivel up and cringe when she's doing it."

"I've been living with my boyfriend for almost two years now. It was great at first, but now all I want is to get away from him. The trouble is that I don't have anywhere else to go. He has a drink problem which is getting worse rather than better. Now when he gets drunk he also gets abusive and violent. I try to avoid him when he's like that because he has punched me a couple of times. But I hate living here and being around him. I just don't know how to get out of the situation."

All these men have to deal with other people's aggression on an almost daily basis. None of them feel that they're coping very successfully. There's no doubt that when you're in a minority of one you can feel like a cornered rabbit if people harass you. If no-one seems willing to support you, it's easy to develop a hefty persecution complex. If you are still struggling with your gayness, you might be having difficulty knowing how - or even whether - to fight back.

Gay people with low self-esteem are at a distinct disadvantage when the going gets rough. If they feel badly about their sexuality, then other people can abuse that vulnerability. Parents who want to keep us quiet or control us can easily turn the screws of guilt; lovers who want to manipulate us can find our weak spots and play them for all they're worth; landlords and employers who want to exploit us can use a kind of blackmail that wouldn't work on other people. Every tin pot bully and swaggering, macho idiot has power over us when they know we're afraid of our gayness.

So what we need to do first is convince ourselves that those who are mindlessly critical of homosexuality (and that's likely to be a sizeable chunk of the population) are wrong. We then have to really believe that it's okay to be gay. If we value our gayness, then it will be very difficult for other people to undermine us by telling us that it is worthless or evil. We will, in effect, have withdrawn permission for them to abuse us.

To do all this we have to look deep inside ourselves. It's a lifetime's work, and you'll never be able to stop making decisions about it. There isn't a point when we will ever be able to say "I'm totally assertive and my self-esteem is secure." Every day some new situation will challenge you to come up with a response - will you be assertive or not. The choice is yours.

2: CHOICES

The development of the gay personality often follows an identifiable pattern, which can take the homosexual person all the way from the first vague inklings of gay feelings right through to the complete acceptance and integration of those feelings. Two researchers have proposed theoretical models charting the way a gay personality develops. One of these is the Australian psychologist Vivienne Cass, and her theory of a six stage process of development is explained in my previous book *Making Gay Relationships Work*. The other proposal comes from an American researcher called Eli Coleman and was published in *The Journal of Homosexuality* (1981-2). His five stage model concentrates more on the later stages of gay development - including the formation of romantic attachments. Mr Coleman's five stages are:

Stage 1: Pre-Coming-Out. At this stage, the individual may not be totally aware of his same-sex feelings because he has made such a good job of suppressing them. He may be vaguely aware that he is "different" from his contemporaries, but not be able to pinpoint exactly what form this "difference" takes. Because of the strength of society's disapproval of homosexuality there might also be an element of denial. A person who is resisting homosexual feelings and trying to pretend that they don't exist may become very adept at making excuses for any 'lapses' he might experience. "OK," he might say after an 'accidental' homosexual encounter "maybe I experiment occasionally with having sex with other men, but it's only because I'm curious, not because I'm gay." Or: "I was drunk, so it doesn't count."

Stage 2: Coming Out. At this stage the individual may be becoming much more aware of his homosexual feelings and fantasies and is probably very confused and frightened by them. It is a period of bewilderment, but there may be the need to tell one or two trusted individuals about the "secret" in order to gauge the kind of reaction the revelation will get. At this stage, the individual will be unwilling to disclose the truth about his feelings to close friends or to family who he thinks might be react badly. The fear of rejection is too intense. He may also make contact with other individuals who share his feelings, and there may be tentative forays into the gay community.

Stage 3: Exploration. During this period the individual will seek out more and more gay contacts in order to explore and experiment with his burgeoning sexuality. It is during this time that he can find positive role models and begin to develop his skills as a lover and intimate friend. Because so many gay people reach this stage much later in their life than heterosexuals (who generally go through this stage in their adolescence), there is a "developmental lag". Gay people might experience their *emotional* adolescence long after their true, chronological adolescence has passed.

Stage 4. First Relationship. Following the initial period of experimentation and exploration in Stage 3, the individual may want to enter into a more committed relationship which combines both romantic and physical aspects. Often these first attempts at relationships don't work because the individual has not really sorted out his feelings about Coming Out. It may also be that he has not finished the explorations and experimentations which are necessary to complete stage 3. If, however, he manages to find suitably positive role models and a support network he will eventually begin to feel more and more comfortable with his sexuality. His experimentation will have allowed him to find out about himself and other gay people. It will be clearer at this stage what the individual really wants from life.

Stage 5. Integration. At this stage, the inner feelings and the public face of the individual become integrated into a single self-image. He is no longer leading a double life and now feels comfortable with his feelings and with the reactions of those around him. The relationships he forms when he has reached this stage are often characterised by a much more mature approach - less possessiveness, more honesty and mutual trust. Relationships formed when the individual reaches this stage have a much better chance of survival.

Some psychologists have suggested that the whole process, from first awareness of homosexual feelings to full integration is likely to take between ten and fifteen years. Naturally some people will move on at a much faster rate than others, depending on the kind of support they may find and the life-experiences they have. There does seem to be some evidence that, as the gay community grows ever larger and more confident, the length of time required to "come to terms" with being gay is getting shorter. There is much more work being done nowadays on support and befriending, which undoubtedly helps more people to move through the stages of development at a faster rate.

But other people become stuck. For some reason - perhaps because they feel isolated and unsupported, or they lack strong, positive role models - they fail to move beyond the first or second stage. This chapter is aimed at trying to help those who have come to a full stop in their development to get the process moving again.

The burgeoning gay man has many choices to make, choices that can progress his journey to emotional integration or, alternatively, bring it to a complete stand still. These turning points can come to us at any time in our life and the decisions we make about them will very much depend on our circumstances at the time.

A small child has a limited number of choices when it comes to re-organising his life and, for his own protection, his parents will make most of his decisions for him. Most adults, on the other hand, have a full range of options to choose from, even though some would deny it. Whenever there is a difficult, possibly life-changing, turning point confronting us, many of us try to avoid it by making excuses. That's because we are wary of change; life is simpler and safer and much less anxiety-inducing if it is predictable and has a set routine. We go to great lengths in order not to disturb that routine. In fact, sometimes people living in the most intolerable circumstances will still avoid change, simply because they prefer what is known and predictable to what is unknown and insecure.

Looking back at some of the letters I received when working on the problem page at *Woman's Own*, I still shake my head in amazement at the lengths people would go to in order to avoid change. I remember quite distinctly a woman whose husband regularly beat her, threw her downstairs and once even tried to suffocate her by putting a plastic bag over her head. Yet still she stayed with him. Although her life was a nightmare, she was reluctant to make any drastic changes because she was even more afraid of the great unknown beyond the clutches of her violent spouse.

And so, even though we are miserable with our existing way of life, we make excuses. We blame our circumstances, we blame other people, we say the time isn't right or that changes could go wrong, leaving us in an even worse quandary. The decision we make is to make no decision, to remain where we are. We choose not to grow but to stagnate. We have changed our opportunity for forward motion into a full-stop.

Two Kinds Of Change

There are two types of turning point. The first tends to come out of the blue, completely unexpectedly; the second is usually the result of one of our own premeditated decisions. For instance, you may have been putting off making changes in your life because there didn't seem any point in doing it. But then, out of the blue, a new person comes along who makes you see things differently. The presence of this special person makes it clear that the upheaval you've been putting off might actually be worth tolerating, for at the end of it will be a big reward. Here is Jeremy, who had such an experience:

> "I was ambling through life in a most unsatisfactory way, with no particular focus. I tended just to let things happen. I knew I wanted a lover, but I wasn't 'out' to the world at large which made it difficult. I didn't make any attempts to find the man of my dreams, I was rather passive about it all. I just had a vague hope that one day he would come along. And believe it or not, he did. I met Hughie at a party - a straight party - and we hit it off immediately. As our relationship grew and matured, I knew that we

were going to be together for a long time. It was through meeting Hughie that I started talking my life in hand and making a few changes. Having him around helped me focus and see more clearly what I wanted and where I was going. I've come out to all the important people in my life, and Hughie and I have set up house together. None of it was easy, but I knew it had to be done in order to move on."

Until he met Hughie, Jeremy had delayed making his choices. His gay life had reached a full stop - a full stop that was entirely of Jeremy's own choosing. He could have taken an initiative in finding the lover he wanted, but instead he waited and hoped. Fortunately it worked out for him, but for hundreds of other gay men that full stop is permanent; the tall, dark and handsome stranger never arrives and options are never actively exercised. The consequence is an unsatisfactory and incomplete life, which need not have been like that. And so, although fate can sometimes deliver our turning points ready made, it's best not to depend on it. A far better option is to create our own turning points and make the most of them.

Of course, having a one-to-one relationship isn't everyone's dream, and if your option is for the single life, you'll still have your own unique set of decisions to make. They may be different kinds of decisions, but the ultimate aim is the same - your happiness, growth and autonomy as a human being.

A Biography of Gayness

In order to demonstrate where these turning points might occur, we can follow the development of one gay man and see how he coped. Naturally we won't be looking at all aspects of his life, this will primarily be a biography of his gayness. He cannot be regarded as in any way "typical" - who is? - but read on and see what you can learn about yourself from Humphrey's story:

Scene One: 1962. Our subject is Humphrey, and he was born in a seaside town on the south coast of England on 25th June, 1962. He was raised in a 'conventional' heterosexual household consisting of a mum, a dad, brother and sister.

When he was five years old, Humphrey - displaying that curiosity which is innate in children - thought it would be interesting to find out what it felt like to be a lady, and so he went into his parents' bedroom, dressed himself in his mother's clothes, smeared his face with her makeup, put his tiny feet into her high heel shoes and paraded around in front of the mirror. While he was doing this, his mother came into the room. She burst into laughter and called downstairs to her husband, "Come and see this!" Father dutifully came upstairs, but was far from amused by Humphrey's juvenile drag act. Papa's face was positively thunderous. "Get those clothes off him - do you want him to turn into a nancy?" Alarmed by the anger in his father's tones, Humphrey became tearful. Father made a sound which indicated distaste and slammed the door as he went out. Mother said: "Come on dear, take those things off, they're ladies clothes. They're not for boys. Boys wear trousers."

When Humphrey was six years old, he began to feel that there was something going on inside him which he couldn't quite identify, but which he knew instinctively he must keep to himself. He preferred to spend his play time in the company of girls, but given that he went to a boys school, he chose for his friends those boys who were similarly uninterested in sports and more interested in gentler, less physical pursuits. The single-sex school also meant that he was often around when the opportunity came for a bit of sexual exploration with his classmates. Humphrey joined in most enthusiastically.

One day he was sitting on the stairs at home when he overheard his mother and father talking in the front room. They were referring to the next door neighbour, Mr Heathcote, who was in trouble with the police. From what Humphrey could gather, Mr Heathcote must have done something really terrible. "I think it's utterly disgusting," Humphrey's father was saying. "I don't know how he could do such a thing with another man." His mother tutted and shook her head. "It's his wife I feel sorry for. How must she feel now that everyone knows she's got a pervert for a husband?"

Humphrey was fascinated by this conversation and longed to know more, but at the same time he discerned from the whispered tones and disapproving manner that this wasn't a topic his parents would be prepared to share with him. As well as the curiosity and excitement about what this terrible thing could have been that Mr Heathcote did with another man, Humphrey also had a slight feeling of discomfort about the vehemence of his parents' disapproval.

He had to wait until he got to school before he found out from his more worldly playmates that Mr Heathcote was a queer and that he'd been caught by the police doing something unspeakable to another man's *thingy* in a public lavatory. Everyone sniggered, and Humphrey thought he had better snigger too lest his friends should realise that he was thinking very hard about what the two men could have meant by playing with each other's *thingies*. After all, they were grown-ups, and grown-ups didn't do that sort of thing. It was beyond his imagination.

By the time he was ten, Humphrey had discovered a little bit more about queers; his school friends were more than willing to explain the full particulars. There was an enormous fascination with all aspects of sex and while they talked enthusiastically and leeringly about girls, they had nothing but contempt for queers. Humphrey, on the other hand, was much more interested in the queers, but had to feign fascination with the various bumps and crevices of girls.

At the age of fourteen, Humphrey had begun to realise that his feelings had a name: not a very nice name. His friends seemed to know all about poofs and queers, and the terrible things they did to each other. There was a lot of contemptuous laughter and people made puking noises when the gory details were gone into. All the boys seemed to be extremely glad that they weren't poofs and congratulated themselves on their healthy interest in girls' tits and fannies.

The problem for Humphrey was that he did not find the same endless interest as his friends did in page three models ("Look, you can see some fanny hair!") and, worse still, he didn't think that what the poofs did was so terrible - in fact, he was discomfited to discover that he quite liked the idea. The realisation was dawning on him that he might be one of those people that his school mates spoke about with such hatred. He quickly came to understand that the only way to protect himself from their wrath was to pretend that he agreed with them on the subject of poofs. And so he joined in his school friends jibes and was as abusive as they were to anyone perceived to be "one of them".

All the same, when his male school friends started drifting away, finding themselves girlfriends to go around with, he just couldn't bring himself to follow their lead. He was only interested in girls as friends and could not regard them as possible romantic partners. Despite the fact that he felt people must be wondering about him, the prospect of going out on "dates" with females seemed alien to him. And so he retired into his shell and stayed at home on his own most nights.

After a while his parents began to ask why he was such a loner and why he didn't go off "courting" like his brother and sister. Humphrey had no answer for them, but felt that they were disapproving and suspicious of his isolation.

Then, one day, in a newsagents shop, Humphrey's attention was caught by a magazine on the top shelf. A magazine called *Butch*. Furtively inspecting the magazine, he discovered it to be full of photographs of naked men, sometimes two or three of them in the same picture. They were looking at each other with frank expressions of desire. He felt the excitement rising in him, and desperately wanted that magazine - even though there was no way he could bring himself to go to the counter and pay for it. And so, for the first time in his life, Humphrey stole something. When he got *Butch* home, Humphrey headed straight for his bedroom and locked himself in. For the next three hours he had a great deal of pleasure using just his left hand to flick through the magazine and his right hand to spice up his fantasies. And, most unusually, when his mother called upstairs to announce that tea was ready he replied: "I'm not hungry thanks, mum."

"Aren't you feeling well, dear?" she'd asked through the locked door. "No," he'd replied, "I think I'll go to bed early." Little did she know that Humphrey was suffering from masturbation fever.

The problem was that there was nowhere he could stow the magazine that would be safe from prying eyes. His mother cleaned his room thoroughly almost every day, and there was no nook or cranny that would escape her inspection. There were no lockable cupboards and, even if

39

there were, a locked cupboard would simply increase his mother's already-high suspicion index. Humphrey began to get panicky - what on earth would she think if she found such a magazine in his room? He was overcome with remorse about having brought *Butch* into the house. How could he have enjoyed masturbating over these pictures - not once, but three or four times? The guilt was like a lead weight in his stomach. And, with anxiety rising, he tore the magazine into little pieces and flushed it down the loo, a bit at a time.

Eventually he began to see that if he was to keep his dreaded secret - and keeping that secret was rapidly becoming the most important thing in his life - he would have to take some steps to cover it up. And so, with all the effort he could muster, he started to go out with a girl called Linda. He chose Linda as his companion because she was plain, dull, unthreatening and demanded little from him. In fact, she seemed so grateful that he was taking an interest in her that she was willing to go along with anything he proposed. Humphrey never made any romantic or sexual moves towards Linda, which she seemed to accept. She did not so much as ask him to hold her hand, and for this Humphrey was eternally grateful.

When he was alone, Humphrey's thoughts were occupied with men, not women. He longed for some kind of contact with someone of his own sex, and yet he knew what the consequences of such a move could be. His parents would find out, his friends would know, his brother and sister would hate him. He had too much to lose and apparently nothing to gain by taking that risk. A curious depression and greyness fell upon his life. He was totally at the mercy of other people.

Scene Two: 1982. And now he was twenty years old, and the sterile relationship with Linda was continuing. His fantasies of contact with other men were not fading as he had hoped they would; he had learned not to stare at those he fancied when he was in the street or on the bus, and he became most adept at concealing what he truly felt. The fact that he had never told the truth about his feelings to anyone meant that the lies, concealment and half-truths tripped from his tongue like second nature. From studying his facial expressions alone, no-one would have been able to detect anything of the yearning that was going on inside him. When he was in the proximity of an attractive male his indifference appeared total, although in reality his heart leaped and fluttered.

A thought had occurred to him. If he married Linda, and tried - really tried - to have sex with her, perhaps these terrible, tormenting feelings would go away. She was such a passive and naïve creature that he knew she would not put much pressure on him if he couldn't manage it. She had expressed a wish to marry - after all, it had been a long engagement. And so, almost gratefully, Humphrey married Linda on his twenty-first birthday. Somehow or other he managed to have sex with her a few times, although he did not enjoy the experience and it did not improve with practice. Somehow or other she managed to get pregnant, and at the age of twenty-two Humphrey was a father.

Despite his joy at having his little son, he was still tortured by the sight of handsome young men in tight trousers. His fantasies when he masturbated were not about women, but always about men. His half-hearted attempts at being a complete husband to Linda had petered out, and they no longer had sex together. Linda didn't seem to mind, she was preoccupied with the baby.

Scene Three: 1986. And now came another turning point in Humphrey's life. At work he met a young man called Harry. Harry was openly homosexual. He made no secret of it, although he didn't "flaunt it" as some people in the office claimed. Humphrey was fascinated by Harry's openness. He wanted very much to talk to him about it, to share his feelings, but Humphrey had never spoken to anyone, not a soul, about how he felt, and it would be difficult to start now.

But, somehow, Harry seemed to have picked up on Humphrey's interest in him, and as the weeks progressed, they began to talk on general topics. They would have lunch together in the staff canteen and occasionally go home on the same bus. Eventually Harry opened the way for Humphrey to tell him the truth. In a conversation over lunch one day, Harry casually said that he knew a lot of married men who were secretly gay and that it wasn't all that unusual. He wasn't shocked by it.

Humphrey knew that this was his opportunity and impulsively he said: "I think I may be gay." Immediately he was sorry. He went red, his heart pounded and adrenaline pumped through his bloodstream. He was panicking. It couldn't have felt worse if he had announced it over the public address system. And yet Harry didn't seem at all surprised, and was taking the news with great equanimity.

"I thought so," said Harry. "Would you like to come round to my flat one evening for a drink, and we can talk about it a bit more?"

Humphrey coughed and spluttered and made his excuses to leave the table. The damned cheek of the man! Just because he'd said he might be gay didn't mean it was an invitation to have sex. And yet, when he got back to his desk and began to calm down, the idea of that evening at Harry's flat - with all its possibilities - came racing into his mind. After all, Harry wasn't a bad looking guy, and there was no need to commit himself to anything. Perhaps he'd just go along for the chat, to be sociable, for a change of scene.

And so next time he saw him, Humphrey made an arrangement with Harry to go along to his flat. He took with him a bottle of whisky, and between them they polished it off. After that, Humphrey felt that whatever he did would be excusable because he was pissed out of his mind. And so when Harry sat on the sofa beside him and put his hand on his inner thigh, Humphrey simply lay back, spread his legs and - at long last - let it happen.

The following day when he got back to work, Humphrey pretended that nothing unusual had occurred the night before. "I'm sorry I got so drunk," he said to Harry, "I didn't say anything out of place did I? I can't remember a thing about it."

Harry smiled a wry smile and said: "No, you didn't say anything." Obviously he'd heard this one before.

As their friendship began to flourish, Humphrey became a little bolder. He saw from Harry that it was quite possible to be a little more honest and open, and that the sky didn't fall in on your head. And yet he was also aware of the vast differences between them. Humphrey was a married man with a child, while Harry was twenty-two and as free as a bird.

Humphrey had become a regular visitor to Harry's flat, but nowadays he didn't need enormous amounts of alcohol to give him the courage to have sex. He actually acknowledged what they were doing and became very fond of Harry. Soon they were talking about being in love - a feeling which was quite new to Humphrey. Although he was fond of his wife, he could never have honestly said that he loved her. But he also felt that there was nowhere for this relationship to go. He couldn't just leave Linda and move in with Harry - to start with, what would his parents say? What would his work colleagues say? He'd be a queer and have to give up everything that he'd worked for. No-one would want to know him. His father hated queers and, it seemed, so did everyone else to a greater or lesser degree.

Scene Four: 1989. One day at work Humphrey was doing some photocopying when one of the typists said to him: "You're ever so friendly with that Harry chap, aren't you? You know he's...well, you know...the other way, don't you?"

Humphrey flushed scarlet and almost choked on his habitual Polo mint. "I think it's disgusting having a poofter working here," said the girl, "They've all got Aids, you know - any of us could catch it. After all, we have to share the same cup with him at tea break. A lot of people are complaining. I think some people have been to see the boss about it. What do you think?"

"Er...oh, yes...terrible," mumbled Harry, not looking at the girl, and trying to gather up his work so he could move away from her.

"Well, what are you going to do about it? Can't you get him transferred somewhere else?"

"I'll see what I can do," said Humphrey, scurrying away in a barely concealed panic. He knew that this woman was completely misinformed about Aids, but his real concern was that she had made the connection between Harry and himself. Although he'd tried to be discreet about their friendship, it seemed that people were putting two and two together. If he wasn't careful, he would end up being swept away by the antipathy that was building up in the office against Harry. Harry, you see, was a challenging and ambitious sort of chap. He didn't suffer fools gladly and he tended not to let things pass for the sake of a quiet life, as Humphrey did. Harry argued with anyone and everyone and he didn't care if he upset them. If they didn't do their job correctly, he told them so. He'd ruffled a lot of feathers and now all those people he had enraged were preparing to get their revenge.

And so Humphrey decided that it couldn't go on like this. He would have to make a choice - Harry or Linda; being a queer or being normal.

After a few nights lost sleep, Humphrey came to his decision. Harry would have to go. There were just too many complications, and the prospect of what his parents would say filled him with terror. He would try again with Linda, he would really try this time. And so he told Harry that he wouldn't be seeing him again. No hard feelings, but he wasn't really queer and he didn't want to continue with their affair.

Harry was upset, and within a month he had found another job and left the firm. This was a great relief to Humphrey, because now temptation was out of his way and he could really make a start with Linda.

But before he could get the enthusiasm going for a sexual replay with Linda, he saw an article in the local paper saying that a gay club was opening in town. It was the first time that there had been such an establishment, and it was causing quite a stir. The local Baptist church was demonstrating against the licensing committee on the local council who had given the club the go-ahead. The local paper dropped through the door, quoting the pastor of the Baptist church in a large headline. "Gays are Evil!" it screamed from the doormat. Humphrey gathered it up and quickly consigned it to the dustbin, Nevertheless, it made him shudder. *Evil* - was he really evil?

Objections to the club turned out to be a storm in a teacup and after a few weeks, most people had forgotten about it and it just settled down to business. But Humphrey hadn't forgotten about it. He was missing Harry, missing the affection and the sex. The old, desperate feelings were coming back again. He would wake up in the night with his arms outstretched, disturbed by a vivid dream about a handsome young man.

The prospect of this club, and the people who would be there, began to torment him. Several times he drove past the building which housed it, just to see what it looked like. He did this until he could contain his curiosity no longer, and one night he wore his largest coat, with the high collar that could be turned up to hide his face, and went along to the club.

Once inside he realised that there were an awful lot more gays in his town than he had realised. He stood at the bar drinking and - well, there's no other word for it - he *lurked*. Men danced together and women kissed each other. Humphrey felt very uncomfortable in such an environment, but at the same time there was something about it which reassured him. And it wasn't long before a youngish man with a pony-tail and ear-rings struck up a conversation with him. Humphrey was self-conscious at first, but there was no doubting that the young man was very attractive. Soon they were in his car, on their way to the young man's home where, once again, Humphrey experienced the kind of love-making that meant something to him.

Scene Five: 1990. Humphrey now had a large circle of gay friends which he had met at the club. There was no problem finding sexual partners because he was a good-looking man, but he had great difficulty making any kind of deeper relationship with any of his contacts. After he'd been to bed with them once or twice, he found that he lost interest and wanted to move on to someone else. However, the gay community in his town was relatively small, and so even though they turned out not to be great love affairs, many of Humphrey's sexual partners developed into close friends. He envied their lives - few of them had married, and most of them were better adjusted to their sexuality than he was.

Many were closeted in certain areas of their life, but open in others. A few, it has to be said, were even more miserable than he was. He saw them in the club, drinking themselves into a stupor each night, buying drugs or trying to gain attention by being shocking and outrageous in ways that, to Humphrey's eyes, were nothing short of pitiful.

He was spending more and more nights away from home, and although Linda had grown more distant, she didn't question him very much about his activities. She seemed reconciled to his neglect and accepted whatever feeble excuse he came up with.

Then one day, who should come into the club but Harry. Humphrey was very glad to see him again, and Harry, in turn, decided that he could forgive Humphrey for his behaviour at work. And so they struck up their friendship again. This time it was different, Humphrey was more relaxed and able to enjoy Harry's company. They went all over the place together, to football matches, to restaurants, the cinema, and sometimes they just sat in Harry's flat holding hands and watching television. Once more Humphrey was approaching the stage where he felt he would have to make a choice - between Linda or Harry, convention or possible alienation. He talked it over with Harry at great length. "You know I'd love you to come and live with me," said Harry, "we could have a great life together. But I'm not going to make the decision for you. It's entirely up to you."

And so, once again, Humphrey tossed and turned, lost sleep, couldn't eat and eventually - unable to stand the strain any longer - simply said to Linda: "I'm really sorry to have to tell you this, Linda, but I'm in love with someone else."

Linda didn't look particularly shocked by this news. "Is it a man or a woman?" she asked.

"A man," said Humphrey.

Linda put her arm round him and said: "I'm so glad you've told me. I think I've known about it for some time now. At last we can be honest with each other, and we can get on with our lives." Humphrey was positively stunned by the equanimity of her response. It seemed that during his neglect of her, Linda had done a lot of thinking. She wasn't a very demonstrative woman, but she had learned something about life, and her suspicions about her husband had begun to grow; her loneliness had told her that she was never going to get the kind of companionship she wanted from Humphrey. She had come to terms some time ago with the fact that he was probably homosexual. She felt excluded from his life, and had come to regard him as some kind of lodger in the house rather than a husband.

Now that everything was out in the open, she asked him what he intended to do. He told her that he longed to go and live with Harry. Linda was happy for him to do that - now, at least, she would know exactly where she stood, and she would be able to make plans for her own future. She agreed that they should separate, amicably, and Humphrey would contribute towards the upkeep of their child.

Humphrey felt remarkably relieved and was walking on air. Now he would be free to live the kind of life he'd always wanted. However, he came down to earth with a great bump when he remembered that his parents would want to know why he and Linda had separated. There would have to be an explanation.

Linda agreed that she would say nothing about the circumstances of their parting, and that it would be up to Humphrey what he told people. That gave him time to think.

His mother was heartbroken when he told her on the phone that he was leaving Linda but, she said, it was happening to so many people these days that it wasn't really a surprise. She wasn't happy about it, but she could accept that they must both know what they were doing. "There's no point in staying together if you're miserable."

Father was more direct: "Is there another woman?" he asked.

"No, there's no-one else. It's just that we both think this is the best thing."

"And where are you going to live?" asked his mother.

"Oh, a friend has promised to put me up for a few weeks until I get myself sorted out..." he said. So many lies had tripped from his tongue over the past years that this one didn't even register.

Scene Six: 1991. And so Humphrey moved in with Harry, and they were sublimely happy. Harry's parents came to see them. Humphrey squirmed at the thought that Harry's mum and dad knew all about their relationship. But they were friendly and accepting, and there was no problem. "When are you going to invite *your* parents round?" asked Harry.

Humphrey couldn't imagine behaving in front of his parents as they did in front of Harry's. "The problem is that they don't actually know that we're...well..."

"Lovers?" asked Harry.

"Yes," said Humphrey. "I haven't told them yet."

"They think we're just flatmates? Well, are you going to come out to them? Don't you think you owe it to them to be honest?"

"Honest? Why, what good would it do? It would just upset them - they're very anti-gay."

"So, if they come round here we have to pretend that we're just good friends? Is that the deal?"

"That's not so terrible is it?"

"Humphrey, I've been out of the closet for ten years now, and I have no intention of going back in again. You can tell your parents whatever you want, but I'm not going to tell any lies."

"Well, if they come round, could I just sort of move my things into the spare room and pretend that I sleep in there, and not with you?"

"Do you know what that does to me? I feel like you're ashamed of me. You think our relationship is something disgusting that has to be hidden."

"No, I don't think that way at all."

"Then why can't you tell your parents about it?"

"You don't know them - they'd never understand."

"Well, so what? You've got your own life to live, and if they don't understand that's their problem."

"I'm just worried what they would say, my mother has angina - she might have a heart attack."

"Well, if she doesn't know at the moment, I'm sure she'll find out eventually. Living here with me for any length of time will soon let the cat out of the bag - she knows some of the neighbours, doesn't she? Surely it's better if she finds out from you than someone else."

Humphrey became very worried about this. He knew that Harry was right. This was a small town and the next door neighbour went to the same church as his parents. How long could he keep it secret? And should he keep it secret?

More lost sleep, more missed meals, and eventually Humphrey decided he had to make a move. After all, Harry had been honest with his parents and they'd coped fine, why shouldn't *his* parents manage? Humphrey was becoming much more aware of the kinds of things that gay people have to put up with in their day to day life, the petty discriminations and insults. He was angry, but he didn't quite know what he could do about it. He sent money to various pressure groups and occasionally went to the local gay society to listen to a speaker. All this was fine, but he came to realise that most of it depended on individuals sorting out their own lives. His consciousness was being raised and Harry's arguments about coming out seemed irresistible. At last he rang his parents and said he wanted to come over and talk to them about something important.

It was a nasty experience, but he survived. His mother had wept and clutched her chest, his father had sat in his chair, eloquently silent. After a while he had left them with their grief and come home to Harry, who reassured him that he'd done the right thing. "Don't worry too much, they'll come round. You have to give them time to get over the shock, that's all."

Three weeks passed and Humphrey heard nothing from his parents. He was worried about them, but felt that he must now wait for them to make the next move. In the meantime he was much relieved and saw a whole new horizon of honesty and openness rolling out before him. But then his mother called him at work one day, just to check on how he was doing. She asked if he would like to go round and visit them. They were struggling to understand, they'd talked about it a lot and tried to make sense of their feelings.

It was a difficult visit, all three of them felt awkward, but he could see that mum and dad were attempting to make a new kind of relationship with him. They were going to have to completely rethink their idea of who and what he was. He felt very affectionate towards them, and said so. "Give us time, and we'll really try to understand," his father had said.

Now Humphrey was free of the fear of being found out he could act on the rage he felt about the homophobia he sensed all around him. He became more involved in the gay movement. He joined a campaigning group and started to go on demonstrations and zaps, he became embroiled in the fight for equality. And the more he found out about it, the more angry he became at the injustice and bigotry. He met more and more well-adjusted gay people, and grew in confidence all the time.

He was soon chairman of the gay group and started giving statements to the press and local radio station. His profile was becoming increasingly public, and more and more people knew that he was gay. That didn't bother him because nowadays most of his friends were also gay. He had left his heterosexual friends behind and thrown himself wholly and completely into the gay community and gay politics.

He felt distant from his extended family and from his colleagues at work; the only people who mattered to him were Harry and his gay friends - these people he considered to be his new family. The rest he regarded as actual or potential persecutors.

Scene Seven: 1992. Now he has given up his chairmanship of the gay group and let someone else take over. He is withdrawing from the gay scene, and he and Harry spend more and more time doing other things. He has grown weary of the discos and bars, there seems little point in going there any more. He suddenly finds himself seeking out his family again, and renewing his acquaintance with his son. He feels much more relaxed and at ease in their company now. The wounds have healed and everyone has accepted that the new order of things is here to stay. Linda has married again, and Humphrey gets on very well with both her and her new husband. He is devoted to Harry, and they feel their lives opening up much more. His resentment about the awfulness of heterosexuals is beginning to wane. He and Harry find that they are cultivating all kinds of friends now, straight and gay. People aren't as hostile as he had once thought they were, and many of them have become close and spend a lot of time at their house. Life is good and Humphrey doesn't think about his gayness very often now, it is such an integral part of his life that he just takes it for granted. He still gets a thrill from seeing handsome young men, and a well-turned pair of male buttocks can still make his heart flutter. But he doesn't feel tortured any more. He and Harry have become almost respectable in their own terms.

In the end, Humphrey made it to a state of complete acceptance and integration, but he had to wait until he was thirty years old before he got there. He would be the first to admit that he made a lot of mistakes along the way, and if only he'd had a little more courage - and perhaps a little more support - he could have broken the pattern of deceit and denial much earlier.

Let's go back to Scene Two and the decision to marry. Humphrey knew that he was gay, but he had no positive input to tell him it was OK. His circle of family and friends told him only that being gay was a terrible thing. Although he knew by this time that there were other gay people in the world beside himself, he had an idea in his head that they were all in some way "different" and exotic. He felt that they were outcasts and weirdoes, and nothing at all like him. As so many isolated gay people come to imagine, there are 'them' (the villainous and undesirable homosexuals of popular fantasy) and there is 'me' (an ordinary, regular guy, who just happens to have these feelings). He did not want to be relegated to the outer darkness which 'they' seemed to inhabit. And so the choice presented to him was either to marry or to take another, even more difficult path - that would allow him to explore his gayness. With no real idea of what his life would be like if he were to take the latter option, Humphrey felt that the safer choice would be to marry.

In making this choice, Humphrey was joining tens of thousands of other gay people. There are critics of the gay lifestyle who say that he did the right thing: he had set aside his homosexual feelings and refused to become exiled from mainstream society. But is this true? Had he really refuted his homosexual feelings, or had he simply hidden them away in a dark corner from where they would continue to stage unwelcome and painful raids into his subconscious?

Humphrey knew quite early in his life where his true feelings lay, and yet he was so poisoned against them that he actually felt it was impossible to express them without the accompaniment of crippling feelings of self-disgust. Only furtively and with enormous guilt would he really acknowledge his gay nature.

In the meantime, his decision to marry had also brought loneliness to his wife. He could only be a sort of unwilling companion to her and, as his frustration grew, he wasn't even that. He projected much of his frustration on to Linda and she, too, became a victim of his internalised homophobia.

At this point many gay men give up the ghost and accept that this kind of half-lived life is their lot. They become embroiled in their heterosexual life and literally suppress any reassertion of their gay feelings. Let's be fair and acknowledge that for many gay people in heterosexual marriages there are compensations: many of them have very close relationships with their wives, they have children which bring them great joy and comfort and they enjoy the support and approval of their families and of society at large. The success or otherwise of these arrangements might have something to do with the strength of gay feeling that each individual is experiencing - the position they occupy on the Kinsey scale which we referred to earlier.

If Humphrey's circumstances had been slightly different he might well have saved himself - and others - much misery and uncertainty. If there had been just one positive role model for him to follow, or one person who could have told him about the choices open to him at the crucial time, Humphrey might have found the courage he needed to his feelings instead of running away from them. But that essential reassurance was not there, and so deeply was Humphrey's self-esteem damaged that he did not have the wherewithal or motivation to seek it out. These are extenuating circumstances for Humphrey, and we shouldn't be too hard on him.

The next great turning point came when he met Harry. This was the role-model that Humphrey had needed from day one. If only there had been a Harry earlier in his life who could have demonstrated that being homosexual need not be the end of the world, he might not have needed once again to turn against homosexuality - and in the process against himself. Humphrey felt terrible about what he saw as his need to betray Harry. But this is a consequence of low self-esteem - one bad decision follows another, mistakes pile up. Humphrey simply had no idea how to challenge the homophobia in his office, he had no idea how to put Harry's feelings before his own fear; he was afraid of the momentous change that would follow any admission that he was gay.

These mistakes were proving to be learning experiences. Humphrey had taken the first tentative step out of the closet with his secretive liaisons with Harry. Now, at last, someone else knew about his feelings. His homosexuality existed somewhere else besides the inside of his own fevered imagination. However, when the crunch came, his choice was to put his own need to protect his edifice of lies first and let Harry suffer the consequences alone. And Humphrey felt bad. He knew he had hurt someone who had become very important to him and he was ashamed of himself. It was the single act that was to change his image of himself. He could, of course, have chosen to stand shoulder to shoulder with Harry at that time, he could have told the office bigots that they were misinformed and that Harry was staying. He could have saved himself much further torment by coming out at this time to Linda and his family. Instead, he had reached a full stop. For some people, a full-stop is permanent - it represents a withdrawal from the struggle, not just a temporary pause. Their first tentative and nerve-racked steps into the light have been unbearably painful and so they withdraw back into the closet, close the door and nail it up. They have created for themselves a permanent prison from which no further attempts will be made to escape.

For Humphrey, though, the feelings were too strong. He could not bring himself to seal his closet door, and when the opportunity came to peep out again, he took it. He moved on to the gay scene, where a limited expression of his homosexuality was possible - while still retaining his anonymity and some options for retreat.

Once more this is a stumbling point for many people. There are those who use the commercial gay scene as a means of finding sexual release without ever making any commitment to their sexual orientation. People who lead "conventional" lives in the heterosexual milieu may seek release in cottages, cruising areas and gay pubs and clubs. By necessity their relationships with other gay people are short-lived, uncommitted and often undignified. People who are simply using the gay scene as a means of putting a toe in the water with no intention of ever taking a swim reach a full-stop at this point. They move no further. If those men who already feel badly about their sexuality meet other people who are equally unhappy with theirs, then they simply reinforce each other's determination to "stick". Negativity can be contagious for those who are already vulnerable to such feelings.

For Humphrey, though, there was a possibility for growth. As he met other gay people who were happy with their sexuality and were pleased to identify themselves as gay he began to realise that it was possible for him, too. Once more a decision was looming. Was he to remain for ever in this limbo of lies or was he going to make the leap into truth? His decision was made easier by the reappearance of Harry - a man who was at ease with himself and his sexuality.

This was a real turning point for Humphrey, because by chance he had found one of the most important elements to help him repair his damaged self-esteem: a role model or *mentor*. Harry was providing Humphrey with a living example of how things can be, he was giving Humphrey something to aim at. And you can do the same. If you are feeling bad about being gay, make an effort to seek out other gay people who feel good about themselves, and pick up a few tips. Even if you don't personally know anyone like this at the moment, think of someone in public life who provides such an example of positivity in relation to their homosexuality, and try to analyse what it is about them that makes it work. Here is what Humphrey has to say about the influence Harry had upon him:

> "Harry was, perhaps the most important single factor in my making the break. Here was a man who didn't put himself or his sexuality down all the time, as some gay people do. He took his feelings seriously and refused to make a joke about them. Oh, don't get me wrong, he has a great sense of humour, and he can make jokes at his own expense. But they are not jokes that belittle his feelings or his sexuality. He is at ease with himself and with other people, and they tend to respond in kind. He doesn't make a big deal about his sexuality, but he never hides it either. People take him on his terms, and if they can't do that, then it doesn't worry Harry. He moves on. If people disapprove, it

doesn't cripple him emotionally as it used to do me. He isn't afraid of what people think, because he likes himself. I think of myself when I was first coming out. I would constantly check people's reactions to make sure that they weren't getting aggressive or hostile or uncomfortable with me. This, in turn, made people feel they needed to reassure me that I had their approval, and that did nothing for my self-esteem. Strangely enough, this confidence Harry has in himself actually creates respect. Most people take him as he is because he *expects* them to - he doesn't seek their approval. I try very hard to emulate him. I know I can never be precisely like him, and it would be silly for me to try. But I've picked up a lot of his good habits and incorporated them into my own life. I have gained a sense of dignity in relation to my sexuality. You could say that Harry is the hero of my life. He's certainly had a profound effect upon me."

Their love for each other developed, despite its unfortunate history. Harry was wise enough to see that Humphrey needed time and space to grow - it had to be at his own pace, it couldn't be rushed. And yet he was there to offer encouragement and this is just what Humphrey needed.

At last he had made the choice that would help him move towards what he really wanted. It had taken several false starts, but now he was going to live the life that he had longed for all these years. His experiences had taught him that there was enough support now for him to take the risk of coming out. If he was rejected by his family and friends, then there was now an alternative support system on which he could fall back. And this is important to rebuilding self-esteem. With friends who understand the situation, you will have increased power to see it through. If you have a support network of buddies who will listen when you're down, help you through crises, encourage you when you are frightened or make suggestions when you are stuck for an answer, then you have an invaluable building crew for your self-esteem.

A major turning point for Humphrey came when he finally decided that change could no longer be put off. It was a decision that made everything possible for Humphrey. It was difficult, fraught and painful, but at last he had the courage - and the vastly raised self-esteem - to be able to go through with the changes that he knew he had to make. He settled the score with Linda and eventually came clean with his parents, too. He was now free to pursue his life honestly and openly. He was a changed man, more confident, more involved in life. The success of his relationship with Harry was also helping his self-esteem to grow, because this was a relationship which he valued and of which he was proud.

It took him a little longer to work through the anger and sense of injustice that is justifiably felt by many gay people. He became estranged from the heterosexual society in which he had been raised. The years of resentment he had endured made him angry at those who had kept him imprisoned. What emerged was a strong desire to fight back and to help others avoid what he now regarded as his "wasted years". Humphrey had felt that he did not belong in his own life. He felt alienated from his family, from his wife and child, from his co-workers and just about everyone else in his life. He felt like a foreigner in his own country. This was because he was burdened with his "secret life".

But now this anger has dissipated a little in the face of the knowledge that not all heterosexuals are as hostile as the ones he'd encountered. He found that support for his relationship with Harry was there if it was asked for. And although there are occasional setbacks, and the anger still flares whenever he come across anti-gay prejudice, he now feels at peace with himself: so much so that he no longer considers his sexuality to be a problem. In fact, he hardly thinks about it at all, and when he does, he's very grateful for it. And strangely, the feelings of "not belonging" have disappeared. He has connected at last with his parents in a way that he hadn't previously. He was not afraid of them any more because the source of his fear - that they might discover that he was gay - has been removed. He feels closer to Linda because now they have an honest friendship instead of a dishonest marriage and he feels far less tense and defensive at work.

We all have our own story to tell. Humphrey had several opportunities to have the kind of life he wanted, but he missed them because he did not have the means of making the right decisions. He was unable to take the risks that are so necessary to build self-esteem. Those people whose sense of self-worth is high have little difficulty taking risks because they can survive rejection and occasional failure. They do not see their whole being at stake when they take emotional or career risks. They learn from their failures and they go on to take different kinds of risks. Those with low self-esteem are fearful of risk-taking because failure and rejection have quite different connotations for them. They feel that they will be unable to carry on if they are rejected by a possible lover or if some career-move goes wrong. Their low self-value makes them reluctant to move.

And yet only by taking risks will we increase our self-esteem. We must make it a conscious policy to take risks as part of our strategy to feel better about ourselves. Humphrey discovered this eventually. His own risk-taking had been postponed many times because he was afraid of the consequences. It might all go dreadfully wrong, he thought, and so he did nothing and continued to live a life of misery simply because it was all he knew.

Every gay person has a unique combination of circumstances and a completely different set of decisions to make. What will dictate our decision-making policy will be the state of our gay self-esteem, the strength of our gay desires and - to an extent - the opportunities that present themselves or those which we create.

The first thing we have to learn, though, is to recognise these turning points and to be able to look clearly at the options that are available to us when they come along. But, say some readers, it's different for me. I don't have a choice, there are too many pressures on me to leave things unchanged. This is an excuse. *There are always choices.* Whether you choose to make changes is entirely up to you, but the opportunity to do so is always there. Those with damaged gay self-esteem will find it hardest to make the changes that are necessary for them to live a fulfilling gay life. Their self-hatred creates a spiral of negative thoughts. Psychologist Sidney Simon put it this way: "The less you like yourself, the more you hurt yourself. The more you hurt yourself, the less you like yourself. If unbroken, this vicious cycle leaves you stuck while the good life goes on without you. You add new items to the list of things you wish you'd done, but didn't. You observe your life dimly instead of living it fully. Dreams and goals for yourself fade to black."

Potential turning points in our life are generally very clear to us, they are usually accompanied by intense feelings of anxiety, joy, fear, gratitude, sadness or relief. We know that our life is changing, and sometimes there is nothing we can do about it (such as when a loved one dies), but often we can influence or even dictate the direction of events by the choices we make. Sometimes these are negative choices: we just let things happen, or we do something that we really don't want to do (as with Humphrey's marriage) because we want to please other people. Sometimes we resist the demands of other people and make a decision to do something else entirely, only to find that it was the wrong decision which we come to regret.

The answer is to try to analyse more clearly what exactly you want this turning point to bring you. In this instance we are talking about your sexuality. Make no mistake, if you decide that you want to embrace and explore your homosexual nature, it will change your life completely. In the early days it is likely to bring you a great deal of anguish, but if you persevere, it can also bring you great happiness.

As I said earlier, everyone's circumstances are different, and with this in mind I am going to ask you to pause now, take out a piece of paper and write down your own autobiography - more specifically, the autobiography of your sexuality. Be as dispassionate as you can, and above all be honest. It's time now to leave out all the self-delusion and excuses, because although it may be painful to face up to the mistakes you have made in life, it will be from these mistakes that you will learn the most. Write about your sexual feelings and how you have dealt with them through the years. Be explicit if you like - after all, no-one but you need ever see it - and write about the good times as well as the bad.

When it is finished, highlight those times in your life which you consider to have been turning points. Then look at the decision you made at these times. For instance, here are parts of Steven's and Andrew's stories:

> **Steven**: I was finishing college and I knew that the time had come for me to decide whether I would return home and live with my parents again, or whether I would strike out on my own. While I'd been at college I'd met Martin, and we had become

lovers for a while. It had taught me a lot about myself. Martin was going back to live with his parents, and my parents were putting pressure on me to return home, too. My father said he had a job waiting for me in his firm. The trouble was that I knew if I went back to their home I would not be able to express my sexuality in the same way as when I was living away from them. I had to decide which was most important for me - having a job and a secure home or going my own way, with all its uncertainty.

Jeremy: I have always known I was gay, and I've never really struggled against it, but I've never really been happy about it either. When you were talking about it with other gays they'd sometimes say: 'If there was a pill that would make you straight overnight would you take it?' I'd always say yes, yes, yes. And yet I couldn't leave it alone. My whole life seemed to revolve around the gay scene. I would spend every free evening flitting between one gay pub and the next, haunting all the clubs in London, looking for sex. If I couldn't find anyone in the pubs I'd start trawling the cottages. I'd grab the first man who showed an interest. I wasn't very discerning and I've picked up some real creeps in my time. There was something almost perverse about the types I would seek out: rough, seedy - smelly even, and some mornings I would wake up and find myself in bed with some truly horrible individual who I wouldn't have given the time of day to in normal circumstances. I would take them home and we'd go mad, sexually. I'd do anything when I was drunk, and I paid no regard to safer sex. When I think about some of the things I've done I feel nauseous. I would go along with any sick fantasy. God, the number of times I've kicked these people out of my flat and then had to clean the place from top to bottom. Some of them even stole from me. But even so, I'd go out and do the same thing the following night. It was like some kind of compulsion to prove to myself that being gay was as dirty as everyone said it was. I was dreadfully unhappy, and I knew I was committing a sort of slow suicide, what with the drinking and all the unsafe sex. I'm not stupid and I knew I ought to get help because I was so miserable with the way my life was going."

Learning From Your Biography

When the autobiography of your sexuality is complete, think carefully about it, and consider whether another turning point is now presenting itself, or whether this is your opportunity to create one. What is it that you want from life? What is it that is holding you back from achieving this? What decisions have you made so far that have thwarted your ambitions for happiness, and what can they teach you?

Asking these questions is often much easier than answering them, and so the next exercise will involve a little imagination to help you.

On your piece of paper write: Chapter Two: The Future. Now continue the life story of your sexuality, imagining how you would like it to develop. Be as positive as you can, think of the optimum conditions which you would like to apply. Write about your relationship with those who are important to you, and those who you would like to be important to you. Invent characters that you would like to have in your life, and then incorporate them into your description of the future. In this version of your life you can have anything that you want, be anybody that you choose and achieve any goal that you set your mind to. Don't limit yourself by saying: "no, that's stupid" or "that's impossible". This is fiction, so you can write whatever you want. Your second chapter should describe the next five years of your life, and it should end with the words "And they all lived happily ever after".

Other people who have tried this exercise have testified to its effectiveness at highlighting the mistakes that have been made. They have also said that it has helped them see what needs to be done in order to make their lives move in a more satisfactory direction. They have acknowledged that their gay self-esteem has been undermined by years of negative indoctrination, but they are at a loss as to how they can overcome it and move forward. Simply recommending that they come out, or change the balance of their relationship or learn how to feel more comfortable with their sexuality is not enough; they need the tools with which to be able to make these changes. And that is where assertiveness can help. Often those with damaged gay self-esteem have problems breaking out of old patterns of thinking and behaving, they don't know how to improve their communication skills so that they can get the best out of their sexuality.

Here are some tips on changes you can begin to make immediately that will help increase your sense of self-esteem:

1. Change the way you talk about yourself. If you tend to use phrases like "I couldn't possibly - I'm hopeless at that sort of thing..." or "I know you'll think this is silly, but...", or "I always seem to say the wrong thing...", then change them to positive statements that say you meant what you said, that you did your best and that you aren't sorry for everything you do. Ask for things positively. Don't say, for instance, "Would you mind awfully if I..." but "Can I..."

2. **Give yourself a treat when you have tried to be assertive - whether the attempt was successful or not**. My own list of rewards is: a cappuccino at the local Italian cafe, a blueberry muffin, a hot bath, a video, a really nice French meal, a Marks and Spencer pudding, a browse in a record or book shop. Treat yourself whenever you are feeling put upon, when someone has been nasty to you, when you've had bad news, when you aren't feeling well, and after every frightening confrontation which you've tried hard to tackle.

3. **Acknowledge and respect your feelings**. Listen to what they are telling you. If you are miserable because of something that has gone wrong, say so; don't put on a happy face for the sake of other people. And it is well known that repressed anger can cause all kinds of physical symptoms, such as headaches and stomach pains.

4. **Look after your body.** You're unlikely to be confident if you neglect your health. Examine your diet and make sure it is balanced and nutritious; ensure, too, that your life isn't too sedentary - get some exercise. Remember the gymnasiums of the land are packed with gay men making themselves look marvellous. And get enough sleep; the modern gay scene makes great demands on our energy - late night clubs and pubs can soon interfere with our energy and moods if we overdo them. Needless to say, the ciggies and drink need to be carefully watched to ensure they don't get out of control.

5. **Find yourself a positive role-model, someone whom · you admire and who you consider has high self-esteem**. Think carefully about what it is that you like about these people, and then try to analyse how they achieve it. Don't try to *be* that person - that would be self-defeating - but try to pick out their good points and incorporate them into your own behaviour.

6. Find yourself a support network - a group of friends who will help you through difficult patches and who will reassure you when you are wavering. Choose people who are positive about their sexuality and who will not try to dampen your efforts at self-improvement. When you have such a network of supporters, value them and reciprocate when you can.

7. Take risks. There is nothing more effective at building self-esteem than moving out into the world and getting involved. Sometimes you will fail, but that is inevitable. Sometimes you will be rejected, but it isn't the end of the world. Give yourself a pep talk before each risk you take, reassuring yourself that if it doesn't work out, then you'll go right out and take another risk that might work out better. You're bound to succeed at some things you try, and when you do make sure you give yourself a pat on the back and add another building block to your sense of self-worth.

8. Stop catastrophising. Some people excuse themselves from taking risks by predicting dreadful consequences. "I couldn't possibly come out - my family would kick me out, I'd lose my job, my landlord would evict me, I'd be beaten up in the street, my grandmother would emigrate to Australia etc. etc." The truth is that things rarely turn out as badly as you think they will. A friend of mine delayed having an inoculation he needed for an exotic holiday because he had convinced himself that it would be unbearably painful. He put it off and put it off until he could procrastinate no more, at which point he went to the doctor's surgery in a state of near collapse. He was sweating, his heart was pounding and his legs were like jelly. My friend rolled up his sleeve and then screwed up his face in anticipation of the worst pain he could imagine. "Thank you, that's all," said the doctor, and my friend was almost disappointed to realise that the injection had been given and he'd hardly felt it. Nor were there any side-effects.

Don't predict disaster for every risk you take. Prophecies of doom tend to become self-fulfilling.

9. **Don't "yes, but..." your options.** This is a classic tactic employed by those who are resisting changes that would help them. They know that their lives need shaking up, but they are afraid of the consequences of doing things differently or moving on to pastures new. They talk things over with their friend, and the conversation goes like this:

> **Person With Low Self-esteem**: I really need to do something about my life. I feel lonely and taken for granted. I wish I had a lover who I could share things with.
> **Friend**: Well, why don't you try and find someone?
> **PWLSE**: How? I haven't met anyone who I could make a relationship with. All the gay men I meet are fickle. They just want sex.
> **Friend**: Some men want to make relationships. I know lots of gay couples. Why don't you put an ad in *Gay Times* and see if you can meet someone that way? You never know.
> **PWLSE**: Yes, but only weirdoes and failures resort to doing that.
> **Friend**: Well, how about going to the gay pub and trying your luck there?

PWLSE: Yes, but that's a meat rack. They're just after picking up one-night stands.

Friend: Well, why not try the local gay group. They seem a friendly bunch.

PWLSE: Yes, but they're just a lot of political extremists, aren't they? I'm not interested in all that gay rights stuff.

Friend: Well then, what are you going to do?

PWLSE: There's nothing I can do, is there? Life's so unfair.

Don't assess your options with a "yes, but..." attitude. Look at your choices objectively and don't go throwing obstacles in the way just because you're scared of change.

10. Don't be too proud to get help if you are truly stuck. If you feel you need to make changes in your life but you can't see the wood for the trees, talk the situation over with a wise and trusted friend. Or find yourself a counsellor who can, perhaps, help you see things more clearly. Simply putting the problem into words can often show you the way to change it for the better. There is some information in Chapter Ten about finding a counsellor or therapist.

11. A feeling of powerlessness is another major symptom of low self-esteem. Assertiveness can increase your feelings of having more control over what happens in your personal life - and that's powerful. It can also make it easier to effect the changes that you have pinpointed in your biography. It can help you to take the action that is necessary to make your turning point a successful one.

3: INTRODUCING ASSERTIVENESS

Assertiveness: To insist on one's rights and opinions -
Oxford English Dictionary.

At first glance, the dictionary's definition of assertiveness might seem straightforward, but, as we know from our own experiences, insisting on our rights and opinions can be a tricky business. It can bring conflict with those we love and those who exercise authority over us - like our manager at work or the police or courts. Insisting on our opinions being heard can create a lot of anxiety and guilt, especially if such opinions go against the wishes and values of important people in our lives.

A lot of thought and effort has gone into defining assertiveness, and even more work has gone into finding methods by which it can be put into practice. We may want to be assertive in every day situations, but how exactly are we to do it? How do we learn to "assert our rights and opinions" while resisting manipulation from others who might prefer us to keep quiet and stay invisible?

Assertiveness can be useful in helping homosexual people live more open, honest - and, therefore, more healthy - lives. However, once you look at the philosophy and practice of assertiveness, it becomes a little more complex than simply "insisting on one's rights and opinions." To begin with, the rights and opinions of gay people are, for some others, matters of extreme distaste, something to be vigorously resisted. The result can be hostility, aggression and sometimes even physical violence. Homophobia is a powerful force, and often the people who suffer from it are unable to control their reactions. But the fact that they can't stop their runaway prejudices does not mean that we, as gay people, must allow them to dictate our lives. The strength of their disapproval must be met with an equal show of defiance. Their aversion must be met with our insistence on our rights. We are entitled to enjoy the full range of human expression and we must not be bullied out of claiming our identity.

The fight against homophobia is on many levels: campaigning and demonstrating on the street are the most visible, but the most effective weapon we have against the attacks of our would-be oppressors is our own self-esteem. If each one of us loves ourselves as *a gay person,* then we are impregnable. Our enemies may beat us up, spit at us and abuse us, but if we love ourselves they will be unable to make any inroads into our self-esteem. We'll just pick up the pieces and carry on loving ourselves and each other.

The utilisation of the behaviour system called assertiveness can make our personal battles a little easier. In the process of fighting and often winning these battles we build up our self-esteem little by little. The overall effect is to make life better not only for ourselves, but also for other gay people.

Although we might talk about assertiveness *techniques* we are not just referring to a set of tricks or manoeuvres to get our own way, we are talking about a total rethink of the way we behave in relation to ourselves - particularly that part of ourselves which is our gayness - and other people. Changing behaviour is notoriously difficult, but it can be done if you are patient and persistent. The rewards of making the effort are pretty spectacular: a whole new and more effective you.

Assertiveness: What It Is And What It Ain't

To better understand assertiveness, perhaps it's as well to say what it isn't.

It isn't aggression.

It isn't intolerance.

It isn't violence or manipulation.

It isn't shouting or antagonism.

Some people claim they are assertive because they can intimidate others with a loud voice or belligerent manner, but that certainly isn't assertiveness.

Being assertive simply means doing what you want to do, saying what you want to say and being who you want to be - without apology, explanation or having to justify yourself. It also means you can do these things without trampling on the rights of others or being upset because you don't have the approval of the whole world.

Lindsay Knight wrote the following about assertiveness:

> *What is the difference between being assertive and being aggressive? The simplest explanation is to imagine being the recipient of both ways of behaving; the person being treated aggressively feels put down, a loser (unless he or she is aggressive in return), shown no respect or empathy as a fellow human being. But if you are dealt with assertively you are treated as an equal - even if the other person is someone in authority over you - and however strong the confrontation, both sides retain their self-respect and demonstrate their respect for each other. In the most difficult of confrontations you can, through*

being assertive, stand up to someone but not at their expense.

Assertiveness has also been defined by Stanlee Phelps and Nancy Austin as "a lifelong process which promotes equality in relationships and preserves self-respect." In other words, you are treating other people as equals and, through your behaviour, demanding that they treat you likewise. Not only do you keep your self-respect, so does the other person.

But, you might say, by these definitions, I'm already assertive; I get what I want and I say what's on my mind. I do this without being aggressive or pushy, and I don't trample on other people in order to function effectively. I am socially skilled and I don't have problems holding my own in social situations.

If you can say this honestly, then you are doing well. But what about that area of your life that is connected with your homosexuality? How honest and assertive are you then?

That's a very difficult question for most gay people to answer - after all, we all behave differently in different situations. It's highly unlikely that we'd speak in the same way to our lover while enjoying a bedroom romp as we would if we were being disciplined by our manager for being late for work.

Some of us get nervous in the presence of authority figures, stuttering and stumbling if we have to talk to, say, a policeman or a doctor. We might be perfectly well able to hold our own when giving our orders to our subordinates at work, but then turn to quivering jelly if we suspect that our family might be getting suspicious about our sexuality.

Even the best-adjusted of us will, at some stage, be evasive about our sexuality, not only about the details, but about its very existence. You can always tell when someone is feeling bad about being gay because if you ask them whether they've come out to their straight friends or their family, they'll get angry and say: "It's no-one else's business. Why should I tell them about my sex life, they don't tell me about theirs."

Oh really? Only a moment's thought will let you see that heterosexuals make statements about their sex life all the time - even if they don't talk about it directly. They wear wedding rings ("With my body I thee worship"); they take their children for walks ("Where did I come from mummy?"); they leer at each other and make lewd comments in the street. Sometimes they live together "in sin", which presumably means they do more than wash the dishes together.

They may not tell you that their favourite sexual position is "69", or that they have sex once a week (or once a month or, God help them, once a year), but they can certainly make it clear that they have a sex life of some kind. This also allows them to talk openly about their partner, about their life together and about their aspirations for the future. It gives the rest of their family a chance to support them and to join in their joy and celebrations like wedding anniversaries. When a gay person shouts at me that "it's nobody's business but my own," I wonder what kind of vacuum he inhabits. If he's going to have good quality relationships with other people - particularly his significant others - then surely it has to be their business too? What kind of relationship can it be that's built on a pack of lies and evasions?

So let's take a little test that will help us be better able to assess how assertive we are with our gayness. Rather than talking in the abstract, we'll go through some specific situations. As you read the following questions, try to put yourself into the scenarios they describe. Although there is an element of fun in this questionnaire, it can also teach us something about our attitudes. Be honest about what you would do.

1. You are sitting in the staff canteen with your work colleagues, when one of them suddenly begins making crude and insulting remarks about a known gay person who works in another department. Do you:

a. *Keep quiet and give no indication that it has any relevance to you?*
b. *Let him know that you find his remarks offensive?*

2. Do you consider your homosexuality to be:

a. *inconsequential and irrelevant to "real life"?*
b. *an important part of your personality to be shared with those people who are close to you?*

3. If you had strong religious feelings and your church told you that the practice of homosexuality was sinful, would you:

a. *Become celibate in order not to offend church teachings?*
b. *Actively question the dogma and try to find a compromise?*

4. You come upon a gay rights parade while out shopping with a straight friend. Your friend says: "They make things worse for themselves by drawing attention to it. If they kept quiet, no-one would bother them." Do you:

a. *Agree?*
b. *Disagree?*

5. You are at a party when an attractive stranger starts a conversation. You would like to get to know him better. Do you:

a. *Become tongue-tied and silent?*

b. *Let him know that you find him attractive and would like to get to know him better?*

6. You've taken your handsome stranger home. You're both ready for a night of passion. He indicates that he wants to have anal sex, although you don't have any condoms. You've promised yourself you'll never do it. Do you:

a. *Go along with your partner's wishes because you are desperate to have sex with him and don't want to jeopardise your opportunity?*

b. *Tell him calmly, but firmly, that you aren't prepared to have unprotected sex, even if it means he loses interest or is offended?*

7. You want to tell your family you're gay. You've told your mother but she implores you: "Don't tell your father, the shame would kill him." Do you:

a. *Agree with your mother and keep quiet?*

b. *Tell your father anyway, because you judge he's strong enough to cope and total honesty is the only way?*

8. Your boss finds out you're gay and sacks you. You feel you've been unfairly dismissed. Do you:

a. *Go quietly because you don't want any more fuss?*

b. *Tell him you intend to fight and seek legal advice?*

9. Your neighbour informs you that when she was passing your house, she glanced through the window and saw you and your lover kissing. Although she assures you she doesn't mind for herself, she wouldn't want children to accidentally see you, in case they were 'corrupted'. Do you:

a. Promise to draw the curtains in future?
b. Tell her that there really was no justification for her peeping through your window?

10. Traditionally at Christmas you spend the holiday with your parents, but this year you want to stay at home with your new lover. Your mother makes a tearful protest saying the family feels hurt and slighted that you have decided to abandon a Christmas tradition in order to be with a 'stranger'. Do you:

a. Go to your parents home as usual, even though you don't want to be there, just to save the hassle?
b. Tell your parents that although you've enjoyed previous Christmases with them, you'd really rather spend this Christmas with your lover?

11. You're walking past a building site with a straight friend when a workman shouts: "Hello Ducky, how are things in queer street?" Do you:

a. Try to ignore the remark, but feel sick and humiliated?
b. Let the remark roll off your back and think nothing of it?

12. You are living in a relationship with another man, whom you love. The trouble is, he thinks it's OK to have sex with other people outside your relationship, even though this makes you extremely upset and jealous. Do you:

    a. Tolerate his behaviour, even though it hurts you and you're afraid you'll lose him if you object?

    b. Tell him how you feel and ask to talk the matter over so that you can come to some kind of understanding?

If you honestly answered all these questions with **b**, then you can congratulate yourself on being assertive in your gay life as well as in life in general. But would you have been able to deal with all these situations without once losing your temper or being consumed by guilt and the feeling that you'd been selfish and hurt someone? Even though you are prepared to do what you consider to be right, can you do it without experiencing that niggling sensation that, when it comes to your sexuality, other people's needs and opinions are more important than your own?

Have you ever felt that when you stood up for your homosexuality, you were being petulant and unreasonable? Do you ever feel that you're being - as disapproving straights so often tell us - strident? Do you come away from such confrontations feeling depressed and isolated? Be reassured that you aren't alone - it's a common sensation which most gay people have experienced at some point in their life. The good news is that such feelings can be challenged and overcome.

But, I hear doubters saying, surely this attitude must inevitably lead to aggression. If we are to stand up all the time for our sexuality, in all circumstances, regardless of what others say or do, we are usually going to end up violating their feelings or rights. If we keep insisting, for instance, that fundamentalist Christians are absolutely wrong in their interpretation of biblical condemnations of homosexuality, then aren't we going to offend them? Don't they have the right to believe whatever they think is the truth, just as we do? Aren't they entitled to respect and dignity too?

Of course they are. They have every right to interpret scripture in any way they want, and to be as disapproving as they like. That doesn't mean that what they say is beyond criticism. They will often say that their religious sensibilities have been offended if they are contradicted, but at the same time they don't hesitate to use the most offensive language in relation to homosexuals. We are, they claim, nothing less than "an abomination."

It is when people such as evangelical Christians try to take action which interferes with the lives of gay people that we have to challenge them. For instance, in the London borough where I live, the local council introduced an equal opportunities policy for its workers. This policy sought to protect those of its employees who were disadvantaged by acts of prejudice and discrimination: those from ethnic minorities, women, the disabled and lesbians and gay men.

A local fundamentalist group objected most strongly to the inclusion in the policy of lesbians and gay men. The group even went so far as to get its pastor elected to the local council so that he could challenge the policy. He was successful in his endeavours, and now this particular borough offers no specific protection to its lesbian and gay employees.

I felt obliged to speak out against the activities of this group, even though it claimed to be "offended" by some of my remarks. I, on the other hand, was not supposed to take offence at their implication that I was, by virtue of my homosexuality, evil.

I repeat, I don't mind what these people believe, but I do mind if those beliefs cause them to interfere with the welfare and human rights of others. I felt an assertive challenge to their activities was in order, and that is what I did. I used no gratuitously offensive words and my argument was intended to be rational and constructive.

So, even under severe provocation, I am not advocating that you trample on other people's sincere beliefs and feelings. At the same time, you should never lose sight of the fact that their feelings are no more important than yours.

Occasionally there will be a deeply personal aspect. For instance, although you may want desperately to tell your parents you are gay, you may fear for their health if they find out the truth. I often hear gay men saying: "Why should I burden them with this at their age? What good would it do?"

I'm not going to say that you should do it anyway. You should make your own mind up. But it is possible you're making excuses, and that's different to genuinely fearing for your parents' welfare. We'll go into that issue in chapter five.

Compromise, too, can be appropriate in some circumstances, and we shouldn't fix in our mind that we have to be assertive all the time - sometimes it would be foolish or even dangerous to insist on our rights and opinions. What we need to be able to do is tell the difference between the sorts of compromises that are reasonable and convenient at a particular time and those that undermine our self-respect. For instance, you might decide to button your coat over your "Queer as Fuck" T-shirt late at night on public transport because you don't want to be beaten up by thugs. This decision might leave you feeling frustrated, but the compromise is justifiable.

On the other hand, suppose you were being evicted from your flat by an anti-gay landlord and you wanted to fight the case. At the same time, your parents are pressuring you to leave quietly and not draw any further attention to your "guilty secret". If you satisfy your parents' demands, and fail to stand your ground in the face of this injustice, you'll be angry with yourself and with them. You haven't done what you felt was right because somebody else thought it was wrong. And that's a compromise that isn't acceptable.

Assertiveness and self-esteem are closely linked. If we don't have much gay self-respect, people will soon pick up on it, and they will take advantage of it.

A lack of self-esteem can show itself in many ways, not all of them obvious. Let's meet a few gay people who lack a good opinion of themselves, and see what it has done to them:

Cyril Shy: Cyril is a reticent soul, painfully shy and quiet. When he talks to you his eyes are constantly cast to the ground and his voice is generally so soft that, after a couple of minutes, you begin to wonder whether your ears need syringing. Cyril doesn't get out much, preferring the unthreatening company of the television set. The television set won't reject him.

Cyril is very angry with himself and very lonely. He knows life is passing him by, but he doesn't know how to break out. He has a rich fantasy life, and often imagines what it would be like to have a lover of his own, but he seems incapable of doing anything to make that dream a reality. Cyril is what is known as passive. Passivity is a means of coping with difficult situations - avoiding them is easier than sorting them out by honest communication. Passivity can sometimes be interpreted as aggression - passive people can manipulate just as effectively as those who are aggressive. A person who sulks, refuses to talk or avoids confrontations can be just as hurtful as one who bullies and blusters. A passive-aggressive person might feign helplessness in order to get another person to do what they want them to.

Nigel Niceguy: Always smiling, always pleasant and never argumentative, Nigel will do a favour for anyone, any time. Need a fiver? Ask Nigel, he'll be only too pleased to lend it to you. He never seems to ask for it back, either. Got a headache and want to leave the party early? Have a word with Nigel, he'll give you a lift home, and he won't complain about being dragged away from the festivities just as they are getting going.

Nigel always seems to agree with you and share your opinions. He will always take your side. He's rather like a chameleon - wherever he is, he changes to fit the circumstances. It's difficult to know what he really thinks about anything because he always thinks what you think.

Underneath the relentless pleasantry, though, Nigel is a seething mass of anger. He knows he's his own worst enemy, but he daren't change because - well, people might not like him any other way. Nigel is another example of passivity in action. He avoids his real feelings by constantly supplicating them to those of others.

Thomas Temperamental: Quick to anger is Thomas, on a short fuse, full of fury. It's very difficult to talk to him because if you put a foot wrong he'll jump down your throat and tear you off a strip. He's a stickler for detail and doesn't like people getting things wrong - he tells them in no uncertain terms if they do. He's often frowning and his grim countenance intimidates people. Those who've felt the rough edge of his tongue tend to give Thomas a wide berth. There is a pleasant guy in there somewhere, but he's submerged under all this bluster. Thomas is considered by some people at work to be a good boss because his colleagues are afraid of him. Thomas feels inside very lonely and rejected. Thomas, is, of course, aggressive in his approach to life. He breaks the rule of assertiveness that says that other people's feelings and needs should be taken into account and respected.

Sidney Screamer: Sidney has decided to take the over-reaction route to coping with his homosexuality. He knows he's gay, and he knows that people are perfectly capable of rejecting him for it. As a result he rejects them first. Sidney *screams* his way through life, flapping his wrists, calling his male friends "her", wearing make-up and semi-drag. He mocks other people before they have a chance to mock him. He is so outrageous that making comments about his sexuality seems almost irrelevant. "Don't bother pointing out that I'm queer," he seems to be saying, "I know it".

By behaving in this exaggerated way, Sidney drives away a lot of people who would make potential friends. To be honest, many of them find his one note rather tiresome after half an hour or so. His homosexuality has become a barrier and a protection for Sidney just as impregnable as the closet is for others. Of course, for many young gay people, a "screaming phase" is an essential part of the exploration period of coming to terms with their sexuality, and is harmless as a method of trying on various gay personas until finding one that fits. Others feel they are making a political statement by flaunting ridiculous stereotypes in the faces of our oppressors. All this is legitimate, but it should not be confused with using this behaviour as a means of postponing creative change.

Most of us have a little of each of these characters in us at different times and in different circumstances, but when one becomes dominant, we can be fairly sure we aren't happy with ourselves. We don't function well in the world; we either sacrifice ourselves at the altar of other people's needs or we drive them away with our bluster, self-centredness or unapproachable mannerisms. In mastering assertiveness we can minimise these destructive elements of our personality and find ourselves getting on better with people at all levels. In turn, our own estimation of our worth rises dramatically. We'll look more closely at passive, aggressive and assertive behaviours in the next chapter.

Applying assertiveness to those areas of our life which concern our sexuality is what this book is about. We might already be very adept in other areas of life: management skills, friendship-making and family interaction - but find that these skills don't run to being honest about our sexuality.

Let's keep things in proportion - being gay isn't all-important, but neither is it something that can be relegated to the status of an inconvenience. If you go through your life imagining that your sexuality is something to be isolated and sometimes "indulged", you will be lumbering yourself with continuous frustration. Your sexuality can only be considered a non-issue when you've completely come to terms with it. Until then, it might well prove to be a source of continuing anxiety. Being assertively gay will allow your sexuality to take its rightful place in your life.

Turning Over A New Leaf

Presumably you are reading this because you think things could be better and you are hoping that assertiveness will help. Well, it can, so long as you are prepared to put in the work needed to master the techniques and to absorb them into your every day life. Luckily there is an opportunity to practise being assertive just about every moment you are with other people. Remember, assertiveness is not about being selfish; it is about communicating your needs, opinions and feelings effectively, while at the same time respecting the needs of others. You will learn how to say 'no' without feeling self-conscious or fretful. You will be able to put your point of view without needing to have it approved. It means that it will be easier to bring your sexuality out of its hiding place and give it the place of importance it deserves.

In order to be successful at our endeavours, it is better to start with small and less threatening tasks. Leave the big coming out scenes or the major confrontations with your lover until you've understood and assimilated assertiveness.

And don't just take my word for it. Go to the library or book shop and read a few books on general assertiveness. They all have their own angle on the subject and you can learn something different from them all. Start to apply the principles in small-scale situations: sending back shoddy goods, refusing to do things you don't want to do, not allowing other people to use emotional blackmail to manipulate you. These are projects with which you can challenge yourself. They will help you understand how assertiveness works and they will help build your confidence as you progress. Then you can begin to look at those parts of your life connected with your sexuality and see how those same techniques can be employed to improve things.

At this early stage, try to keep a record of what you're trying to achieve and write down whether each attempt to use assertiveness was successful. If not, you can then analyse what went wrong. For instance, when I was trying to incorporate assertiveness into my life, I was having problems saying 'no' to demands that were being put on me. Because I was writing a regular column about press attitudes to homosexuality in a magazine, I was often approached by students or television researchers to provide them with information and research for their own projects. At first I was happy to oblige, and would do my best to find the information they wanted. Soon, though, the demands for research material were outstripping the time I had available to attend to them. However, I found it very difficult to say: "I can't do this for you, I have a living to earn." I began to get resentful when letters arrived from students who had set themselves the task of writing a paper on "Media Attitudes to Lesbians and Gay Men." Typically, the letter would read like this: "Please send me all the information you have concerning the above topic as soon as possible." They hardly ever even enclosed a stamp for a reply. At certain times of the year, three or four of these letters would arrive each week. I would be annoyed, but would feel that I was letting the side down if I didn't do as I was bidden.

TV and radio researchers, too, would ring up - the epitome of charm, it has to be said - and ask very politely if I could provide them with some juicy press clippings for a programme they were doing, and could I possibly manage it in the next half hour.

They, of course, were on fat salaries and they got their names on the credits, but muggins here had to make do with their grateful thanks. But what could I do, committed as I was to the promotion of gay rights at every opportunity? Anger was rising, and I knew that I was going to have to draw a line on the demands that were being made on my time. I wanted to use that time to write, not run round after people who were perfectly capable of doing their own research. But how was I to say 'no' without curling up with guilt or feeling rude?

I had analysed what was happening, and I decided that I was, in a polite kind of way, being exploited. And that had to stop. And so, when the next researcher rang up, I was determined that I wasn't going to be pushed into doing unpaid work that I didn't really have time for. The conversation went something like this:

"Hello, Terry, we're working on this programme about how rotten the press are to lesbians and gays, and we know you've spent a lot of time studying it. Really, what we want to do is have some examples of particularly nasty headlines to illustrate it with - could you come up with a few we could use? Just half a dozen or so. If you could just give us the dates and the papers they were in, we'll find them out."

"That will take quite a lot of time. It will mean me going back through my records."

"That's OK - we'll call you back in an hour, would that be OK?"

"Well, I..."

"That's really kind. I didn't really know who else to ask - you're the only person who does this kind of thing, and you're so good at it."

"Oh, I..."

"Right then, I'll get back to you in an hour - if I've got time."

When I put the phone down I was shaking with anger. Hooked again. So much for good intentions. Instead of doing what I should have done and waited for the return call in order to say: "I'm sorry, I don't have the time to help you with this. I have to earn a living."

Instead, I unplugged the phone and left it unplugged until I judged that their deadline had passed and they wouldn't ring back.

Now I was even angrier - not only had I failed to say no, I had taken the coward's way out and simply avoided the situation altogether, leaving it unresolved. Soon some other researcher would call and I'd be in the same pickle. So, I took time to think through what was going wrong in order to try and put it right the next time. I decided that I would have to be up front from the beginning of the conversation and not be drawn into the details. The 'no' would have to come fairly soon after the request was made; the later it was left, the more difficult it would be to say.

Nowadays I exchange civilities and then tell them that I charge a £50 consultation fee and if they don't want to pay that, then I can't help. I feel that is fair, but it took me a long time to be able to say it and not feel guilty and grasping. After all, I have a right to say 'no' whenever I feel like it, and I don't have to feel guilty. Similarly, I have decided that I will only reply to students who send in a stamp, and only then to tell them politely that I have to decline their offer of extra work - which they could do themselves with a little effort. What a relief.

Persistence Is The Key

It won't be all smooth sailing to begin with (or later, come to that). You will have failures from time to time, just like I did. Don't let these dishearten you. Regard set-backs as learning experiences and analyse what went wrong. Radically changing your approach to life is not something that can be achieved overnight, so be patient and forgive yourself your mistakes.

Most of all, don't imagine that you need some special talent in order to be assertive. For some people it seems to come as second nature and they appear to sail through life with an apparently unshakeable belief in themselves. Why some people seem to be 'naturally' self-confident, while others have to work at it, might be due to a number of factors. Most importantly, that person might have been brought up by parents who taught their child to think of himself as innately important. Most of us, unfortunately, have been raised to think the opposite about ourselves. But recognising our hang-ups is the first step to overcoming them, and you don't need a single GCSE in order to do that.

The following words were written by a psychologist, Dr Paul Hauck, and they should give pause for thought to anyone who doesn't feel in control of their life:

> *"Not to be strong and assertive when your important desires are at stake, leads to a wasted life, physical and emotional slavery, and serious physical and emotional problems."*

That need not happen to you. So let's begin the journey that will save us from the physical and emotional slavery to which the non-assertive are prone.

4: ASSERTIVENESS TECHNIQUES

In this chapter we'll look at some of the techniques of assertive behaviour that can be learned and then used in many of the circumstances we find difficult to cope with. In later chapters we'll consider how these techniques can be adapted specifically to situations which affect our sexuality. We'll find that, by approaching them assertively, those frightening turning points in our lives can be more effectively handled. Instead of seeing our all-important choices as being confusing and terrifying, we'll come to see them as great opportunities to change things for the better - and be in a better position to make those changes.

We won't, however, be able to shake up our lives without affecting other people. Most of us have family, friends or lovers and most of us have jobs that bring us in to contact with other people and it follows that if we are contemplating making profound changes in the way we behave, then those around us are sure to notice. They may not approve of our new way of behaving, so we may have to negotiate with our 'significant others' about any new order we wish to create. Sometimes those negotiations can be difficult and painful, but assertiveness can help us deal with them more effectively and keep the unpleasantness to a minimum.

Four Essential Points

There are four main points - Golden Rules if you like - to remember when thinking and behaving assertively. They are so important - and we will be referring back to them throughout the rest of the book - that you might consider writing them on a piece of paper and placing it somewhere where you will see it frequently:

> **1.My feelings and needs are at least as important as anyone else's.**
>
> **2.My rights are sacrosanct and it is my first duty to protect and promote them - but not at the expense of other people's rights.**
>
> **3.I am not responsible for other people's feelings, and they are not responsible for mine.**
>
> **4.I do not have to explain my decisions or justify my feelings or actions unless I want to.**

Three Ways Of Behaving

There are basically three ways of behaving in any interaction with other people: passively, aggressively and assertively. Most of us use a combination of all three behaviour-systems depending on the circumstances; the assertive person will be able to freely choose between them. But those whose confidence is less high can feel that they have no choice, that they have no control over events and so deal with their problems in stereotyped and unhelpful ways. They may have found that they get quick results from being aggressive or can avoid taking risks by being passive and so they continue to use these methods; but by choosing to behave assertively, we get far more satisfactory results in the long-run. With assertiveness we don't have to keep repeating painful mistakes or passing up life-enhancing opportunities.

Let's look more closely at each of these three ways of behaving, because it is important that we understand the difference between them.

AGGRESSIVE:

Aggressive behaviour gets results, but those results often come at the expense of other people's dignity. A predominantly aggressive person will often use terms such as "You'd better...", "Hurry up", "Get out of the way" and "Shut up". His body language will be taut and stiff, and his voice will be loud and intimidating. His moods may lurch between anger, resentment, irritation, loneliness or passion. He may lean toward alcoholism. He feels he has a sense of humour, but this generally consists of put-downs, sick jokes, insults and cruel practical jokes; at the same time, he seems incapable of laughing at himself. He will often find it difficult to make real friends - although he may have many acquaintances - and there will be little intimacy in his life.

On the positive side, aggressive behaviour can be useful in the face of threats; it can also be used to gain benefits for good causes; it is useful when strong leadership is required; and it is good for expressing real, justified anger.

Taken to its logical extreme, though, aggression can lead to burn-out, disillusion and self-destruction. It encourages other people to become aggressive and manipulative in return, and life rapidly becomes filled with unpleasant hostility.

PASSIVE:

The predominantly passive individual often comes over as docile, acquiescent, meek, helpless or indecisive. Or he might be excessively charming, agreeing with everything you say and backing up all your opinions. He will appear to have no original thoughts and simply reflect other people's opinions. He is often pessimistic and negative about events around him, and blames himself for things that go wrong. His most frequent expressions usually involve an apology: "I'm sorry to bother you...", "Would you mind awfully...", "It's only me...", "Don't take any notice of anything that I ₅say...", "Excuse me..."

His body language is generally inexpressive, he keeps his eyes down much of the time, wrings his hands, speaks softly and monotonously. He may also have a stooping posture. Alternatively he may try to gain approval by being cute and charming and self-deprecating, always smiling and friendly, never arguing or contradicting. You will find it almost impossible to know what he truly feels.

He prefers life to be predictable and is cautious, avoiding change as much as possible. He is often a nurturing individual, who sacrifices himself to the needs of others - frequently aged parents. He can also be indirectly aggressive - a malicious gossip, preferring to get his way by plotting behind people's backs.

His sense of humour tends to be collusive - he will conspire in cruel pranks or back-biting. He also has a tendency towards sarcasm and cynicism. Much of the passive person's humour may revolve around self-criticism and putting himself down.

Passive behaviour can be useful in some cases - for instance, if you want discretion, or to minimise risks in any situation. People who behave passively are often extremely reliable, and they like to remain unobtrusive. On the other hand, such behaviour can lead to them being victimised - even to the point of martyrdom. They can become depressed and phobic, they might overwork themselves to the point of illness, and they might unconsciously invite other people to humiliate and abuse them.

Strangely enough, though, those we at first label passive might in fact be aggressive. People who are thoroughly "nice" can quite often use their apparent blandness as a cover for extreme anger. Often it is difficult to pin down the source of the aggression when it comes from such people, because it is usually furtive, planned behind your back or in collusion with others. The smiling Mr Niceguy might well be plotting your downfall when you're not around. You'll never get him to slug it out with you face to face, because he'll always tell you that he doesn't like trouble - he doesn't want to fall out with you, he wants to be your friend. He's a dab hand at supporting one point of view in one situation and, if necessary, the opposite in another. In personal relationships, a passive person can find it difficult to express his needs clearly, and might try to have them met indirectly. He might be a sulker, mooching round the place sighing until you manage to guess what it is he wants. Or he might play helpless, giving the impression he needs your support and nurture.

ASSERTIVE:

The assertive person is generally an optimist, who is fair-minded and self-protective. He generally has an insistent streak that helps to ensure that his feelings and needs are always part of the equation. He is not averse to compromise and will negotiate from the point of view that both parties should get at least some of what that they want. He is sincere in what he says and open with his feelings. The types of expression he might use are "I want...", "I feel that...", "Why don't we...", "What do you think?" "Let's talk it over....", "Yes", "No".

His body language is generally relaxed and expressive. He is upright, alert and gives eye contact. His voice is clear, well-modulated and sincere. His over-riding moods are happy, energetic, sad, compassionate, relaxed or poised.

His sense of humour is playful, and he likes to make jokes - but not at the expense of others. He can laugh at his failings without putting himself down.

He is generally a humanitarian, concerned that people should have their dignity respected. He will be organised and try to live within a fair ethical framework (he will not unquestioningly accept someone else's ready-made moral code).

Assertiveness, as we've already seen, can lead people to be more democratic, independent and team-spirited. It makes them better communicators, and better able to cope with criticism. They are able to take risks and to accept intimacy with other people.

The negative consequences are that some people don't like assertive individuals and are fazed by their self-sufficiency. They are also often burdened with high expectations from others.

In the light of this, think carefully about your own behaviour. It is unlikely that you are aggressive, passive or assertive all the time, but if you recognise yourself as overwhelmingly aggressive or passive, then you need to make changes in order to get more out of life.

Communication Is The Key

Assertiveness is basically about honest communication and the expression of genuine feelings. Many gay people have spent a lifetime controlling their feelings and denying honest expression of them. For homosexual people to have been totally spontaneous about inner feelings would have risked exposing to the world what they might have regarded as their "dreadful secret". We spend our most important years learning how *not* to be honest about our feelings and how to hide them; anger, love, sorrow - and even the fear that motivates us can be concealed behind a wall of pleasantry, passivity or bluster. After becoming so expert at suppressing important but inconvenient feelings, we will find it difficult to change the habit. It will not be easy, after all these years of concealment, to identify the real, genuine feelings that need to be given expression. But if we want to be assertive we will have to learn the skill of separating our genuine emotions from those that we use as a smoke screen. We will have to get into the habit of liberating those feelings which we have kept locked away and suppressed.

In the past, we may have put up with a lot of interference in our lives from other people. We have let them manipulate us and make demands on us because if we did not, they might have learned the truth about us. We have, in many cases, colluded with our oppressors to make their job easier. Now we're going to change all that. If we are angry with someone because they are trying to block our progress, then we are going to have to acknowledge and express that anger - terrifying though the prospect might seem. This does not mean "no more Mr Nice Guy", but it does mean that Mr Nice Guy is going to have to find his place along there with Mr Angry and Mr Loving and Mr Silly, Mr Sexy and all the other aspects of our temperament that we have, until now, damped down.

If we are burdened with unsatisfying and unpleasant relationships, which exist simply because they've always existed, we will have to find the wherewithal to let go of them and seek out truly satisfying alternatives. For those who are afraid of the consequences of profound emotional change (and that includes a vast number of gay men), a major reappraisal is required.

So, our new resolution is honesty with ourselves and honesty with other people. We are going to teach ourselves to tell others directly and straightforwardly what we want from them, and what we are prepared to give them in return. To be able to do that effectively, we have to be clear in our own minds precisely what it is we want. For instance, if you have to tell a colleague that his work is not good enough, but don't know how to do it without hurting his feelings, then think carefully about how you could phrase the criticism so that it doesn't sound as though you are condemning the person completely.

"I'm generally very happy with your work, John, but I feel this particular project isn't up to your usual standard" must surely be better than "You're producing lousy work, I don't know why I ever hired you." The first version is kinder, but it lets the other person know how you feel and also lets the person know that you still have faith in them. It is likely to get a much better reaction than the latter. This is the assertive way of doing it: you've said what you had to say, but you have respected the other person's integrity.

The message has to be delivered clearly, directly and with respect. It's no use going round the houses to get to what you want to say, that just opens the way for misunderstanding. A non-assertive way of doing the deed might be: "I've been meaning to have a word with you about something, John, and it's very difficult. I've been looking at your work and...well, perhaps, if you don't mind, we could sit down and look at the details. No, honestly I'm not criticising, don't think that, I mean, you've been doing this job for donkeys' years now and you know far more about it than I do...I just thought you might possibly be interested to hear what I've got to say about this particular project, if that's OK." Beating about the bush in this way doesn't get the message over effectively. You feel frustrated because you didn't tell your colleague what he needed to know, and he feels confused because he doesn't really understand what you're getting at.

Another instance might be if you're feeling frustrated about your sex life and want to suggest an improvement to your lover. Think carefully about what *exactly* it is, so that he isn't left floundering when you tell him. State directly and precisely what it is he needs to know. Don't say: "I'm not happy with our sex life" but: "I love having sex with you, but I'd like our sessions to last a bit longer - can we spend more time playing around before we get round to having our orgasm?"

The first statement could raise all kinds of insecurities and misunderstandings, it would be quite reasonable for your lover to imagine that you're telling him he's completely hopeless in bed, which would be hurtful and unnecessarily cruel. With the second statement, you both know precisely where you stand and you can negotiate from there.

If you want to come out to someone, you can say: "I have something to tell you - I'm gay" or you could say: "I've got something to tell you, but I don't really know how to put it. I know you're going to be upset so prepare yourself, and I'm very sorry to have to do this to you. I expect you can guess what it is, can't you? Shall I make you a cup of tea?" and then leave them to work it out for themselves.

The passive way of telling people what you want them to know, would be to sulk, remain silent and slouch around the house looking miserable until someone says: "What's the matter?" The passive person inevitably replies: "Oh nothing", and continues to sulk, slouch, whinge etc., leaving everyone feeling terrible. The aggressive person, on the other hand, might explode: "It's you and your sleeping around - you're a sex-obsessed traitor and a worthless slut." You've got the message all right, but you're likely to set off an unpleasant and equally aggressive reaction. Instead of leading to a constructive discussion of the problem, it is much more likely to lead to resentment and defiance. Having said that, this response - desperate as it is, is better than avoidance.

Choose precise words and try to avoid vague expressions. If you're trying to arrange to meet a friend, but you can't find a time that you're both free, don't say: "Any time will do" but, "What about three o'clock". If you can't agree where to eat out, don't say: "I don't mind" if you really want to eat at a particular restaurant. Being direct and precise means that there is less scope for misunderstandings. People will know where they stand when you speak to them, and they will respect you more. Stating what you would like doesn't necessarily mean that you aren't prepared to negotiate a compromise if the other person wants something else.

Being direct and straightforward will help build your self-esteem. So, if you're heading for a confrontation or a negotiation, think carefully beforehand what exactly you want from the encounter, and then state it clearly.

Many people with low self-esteem are reluctant to take risks in confrontational situations, they are always the ones who back down. They are often incredibly angry and frustrated with themselves because they don't get their point of view over which results in them being exploited or in doing things that they don't want to do. Avoiding confrontations is the safe option, but it is also the option that gnaws away at your self-esteem. Naturally there will be times when you judge that (a) it would be unsafe to confront someone (perhaps a gang of drunken yobs who are shouting anti-gay abuse in the street); or (b) you don't adjudge it to be worth the expenditure of energy. However, whenever possible, try to stand your ground in confrontations and at least put over your point of view with confidence and clarity.

So, the first rule of assertiveness is: know what you want to say and say it directly, but also say it in a way that respects the other person's dignity and feelings.

Accompany your direct speaking with the appropriate body-language which will reassure the person you're speaking to, while at the same time letting them know you mean business. Sit or stand up straight, look the person in the eye, smile reassuringly, use a level, friendly tone of voice and then say what you have to say. If done in this way, even the most unwelcome message can be delivered with the best chance of a reasonable reaction.

Nerve-racking confrontations can cause our hearts to pound mightily and make our breathing fast and shallow. This, in turn, affects our voice. We might find that we can hardly get enough breath to utter a complete sentence, and this makes us sound faltering and unsure. The throbbing heart can make us sound quavery and petrified. The answer is a simple breathing exercise which can help you overcome this particular problem. Make sure you are sitting or standing upright. Take in a deep breath through your nose and really fill your lungs. Breathe out slowly. Take another deep breath, this time even deeper than the last, and really expand your lungs. Now exhale slowly through your mouth. Do this for a minute or so, twice a day, and it will help strengthen your lungs. You can also do it immediately before a situation which you know is going to make you nervous or angry.

The tone of your voice is very important. Have you ever heard yourself speaking? If not, record a few words with a tape recorder and play it back. How does it sound? Friendly? Unfriendly? Defensive? Bored? Angry? Loud? Soft? Strong? Weak? Think of ways you can make it sound more assertive - that is, strong without being threatening, friendly without being submissive. Experiment with a phrase, such as "Oh really?" Say it into the tape recorder in the following tones of voice: hurt, snobbish, friendly, aggressive, sympathetic, nagging, cajoling, simpering. After playing it back, you will be able to see how you can control the manner in which you speak to people, and thereby influence the way they react to you.

Ask a friend to listen to your normal speech (it's unlikely that you'll be able to speak spontaneously into a tape recorder). Ask him to tell you how you come over - do you end your sentences with questions, as though seeking approval for everything you say? ("What do you think of my new trousers, they're stylish, don't you think?") If you do, make a conscious effort to control it. Speak in statements that sound as though you mean them.

Now think about your facial expression. A smile is recognised universally as a sign of reassurance, and if you are saying something to someone which you think they aren't going to like, you can soften the blow by saying it with an appropriate smile. Like tones of voice, smiles come in all shapes a sizes; you have to choose the one that is right for the occasion. A simpering, obviously phoney smile will not help you get your message over, and a huge grin will not reassure someone that what you're saying is meant constructively. So, it has to be a friendly smile, not too big, and coming as much from the eyes as from the mouth.

The rest of your body can speak volumes, too. Assertive people always keep their head up and look the other person in the eye when they're talking to them (without staring, which can be threatening). They stay relaxed, but don't slouch. They don't wag their fingers, roll their eyes upwards in despair, fold their arms, turn away from people, frown or deliberately stand over people in a menacing way. We'll talk more about body language later, but remember in the meantime that your message will be much more effective if it is delivered in a confident, alert but relaxed way.

So, if you have something to say to someone which they might not want to hear, then remember these points:

1. Think it through first. Think carefully about what exactly it is that you want to achieve by this conversation, and how you can state your feelings and wishes in a clear, unambiguous way. Try not to go around the houses to get to the core of your message, state it directly - while at the same time having consideration for the feelings and rights of the other person. Try to identify your feelings about what is happening, and include those feelings as part of your message. ("I feel angry about the way you broke our date without letting me know"; "I am very sorry that you feel that way").

2. Have a course of action ready to suggest. Don't just criticise and leave it at that, try to be constructive about it.

3. Listen carefully to the reaction. Really take on board what the other person is saying in reply, and respond accordingly. Acknowledge that you have heard their point of view, have considered it and then restate your case gently but firmly, making it clear that you have taken into account what they have said.

4. Try to reach an agreement which is acceptable to both of you. Try to create a win/win solution, where both parties feel they have achieved a little of what they wanted. Compromise is often the most assertive way to proceed - you have to be the judge of how much you are prepared to concede, according to the circumstances.

Of course, with delicate or controversial messages you may not get the response you had hoped for. If you are telling someone something they don't want to hear, they may well respond with hostility or aggression. You have to prepare yourself for this. Don't lose your temper in return, but simply try the message again in another way or at another time. You may have to repeat the message several times before the person acts on it. Be patient and you will succeed.

Don't allow anyone to get you off the track. This is a common trick used by those who are trying to avoid an issue - they will drag in something totally unconnected in order to fog the real topic. For instance, you may be angry at your lover for raising a touchy, private subject at a dinner party. Afterwards you say: "I was very angry when you mentioned that personal problem of mine over dinner. I particularly asked you to keep it to yourself. Please don't do that again." In order to avoid the issue he might say: "You've got no sense of humour, you were a real misery all night."

An assertive person would respond by bringing the conversation back to the topic in hand by saying: "Perhaps I wasn't particularly sparkling tonight, but I was very embarrassed by your remarks about my private affairs and I don't want you to do it again."

As you've seen, being assertive is not always easy, and sometimes it doesn't bring the results we'd hoped for. But at least it gives us the opportunity to express our true feelings and have them heard. Even if we only achieve fifty or sixty or seventy per cent of what we're aiming for, it surely has to be better than nothing at all.

However, writing or saying these things is not quite the same as living them on a day-to-day basis. If you are used to putting your needs second to someone else's or if you find that saying 'no' is difficult, then you will realise that, somewhere along the line, assertiveness might be useful to you. Take, as an example, this hypothetical scenario:

You are at work - where you have not come out to your colleagues - when one of your workmates comes up to you and says: "I was walking by that gay bar in town on Saturday night around closing time, and I saw someone amazingly like you coming through the door. I said to my girlfriend, I'm sure that's the chap from the office, I'll ask him on Monday morning. Was it you?"

Faced with such a direct question, you may become panic-stricken: now he knows and probably everyone in the office is going to know in a few minutes. How do you deal with it?

The non-assertive person might be flustered and say: "no, no, it wasn't me. You must have mistaken me for someone else. I was at the cinema with my fiancée on Saturday night. I wouldn't go anywhere near that bar, the very idea!"

On the other hand, bearing in mind what we now know about assertiveness, you might say calmly: "Yes, that was me." You then have the choice: whether to elaborate on that bald statement or not. The key word here, as ever, is choice.

It is not compulsory for you to explain anything further. Your colleague has no God-given right to know why you were coming out of the gay bar, what you were doing there in the first place, whether you are gay, whether you have a boyfriend or a girlfriend or a live-in orang-utan. But, in a situation like this, many gay people will immediately experience feelings of dismay about being found out. They don't know why they feel guilty, but the shame about their sexuality which they've been harbouring for so long, now comes to the fore. In this situation, the non-assertive gay man might begin to shout and get aggressive, becoming upset and anxious about the whole thing. In getting agitated, he is allowing his emotions to be manipulated. Golden Rule number 3 has been flouted: he has allowed someone else to control what he feels.

Back to the office and the workmate is pressing for more information: "What's it like in that pub? Do you go often? Does the boss know about it?"

If he hasn't begun to shout by this time, the non-assertive gay man might be tempted to try and justify his visit to the pub, making excuses or inventing an elaborate cover-up. At that point, dignity is either lost completely or hangs precariously in the balance. The non-assertive gay man feels trapped and afraid, asking himself "where is all this going to lead?" The assertive gay man, on the other hand, keeps the fear under control, remains calm, refuses to fill in the spaces in the conversation and tells only what he is prepared to reveal.

"Do you go to other gay places?" your colleague is asking, with a hint of prurience and malice in his voice. The assertive man simply remains silent or says something like: "I really don't want to talk about my personal life with you." There is no need to say anything more, however hard you are pressed. You can ignore sarcasm, cajoling or threats. If the pressure continues and you feel some response is necessary, you can use the "broken record" technique. This simply means that you repeat your initial response as many times as necessary in order to deflect unwanted enquiry. The broken record technique in action would go something like this:

"I'm sure I saw you coming out of the gay pub on Saturday night. Was it you?"

"It might well have been. I was in that bar on Saturday night."

"Do you go there often?"

"It's really none of your business, and I don't want to discuss it."

"Why? Are you gay or something?"

I don't want to talk to you about this."

"I've often wondered about you, never having a girlfriend. Have you got a boyfriend then?"

"It's not something I want to discuss with you. It's really none of your business."

"Why? Have you got something to hide?"

"I'm not going to discuss this with you."

This can go on for as long as it takes to give your colleague the message that you aren't going to be pushed into talking about something which is none of his business. To be effective though, it has to be delivered without anxiety or rancour and in a moderate, well-modulated tone of voice.

However angry your colleague might get at the lack of progress, you are not going to get angry with him and nor are you going to fall into the trap of elaborating the original response. Rephrase it by all means, but don't add to it significantly - unless you want to.

There is no need for you to feel that you owe an explanation for your activities; this man has no particular right to have information about you and, therefore, if you don't want to give it, don't give it. But refuse in the nicest possible way, and in that way you'll be much less vulnerable to the intended humiliation.

When you first try this technique (or any other behaviour which is different from your usual style) you are likely to feel anxious. If you are used to giving in to other people's demands without an argument, then suddenly resisting can be a terrifying ordeal. Whoever you are talking to might try the usual manipulations on you - guilt, intimidation, power play - but it is up to you to resist these.

If you've used the broken record technique, for instance, to say 'no' to your boss when he asked you to work late one night when you had an important date elsewhere, you might still feel guilty. ("Perhaps I let the boss down by refusing to stay over this evening, perhaps it will make a lot of extra work for other people. Perhaps I was being selfish by putting my own needs first.") Naturally you will have to weigh every situation individually and come to your own conclusion. In this instance, you did not judge that the work your boss was asking you to do was as urgent and essential as he said, and so you saw no reason to cancel your important social event. Remember, your priorities are as important to you as his are to him. Ignore the voice of guilt that says that people depend on you and therefore you have no right ever to say no to them. Endure the feelings of guilt and recrimination for the time being. The anxiety can be mitigated by relaxing and breathing easily - techniques for which will be explained later.

Dealing With Authority Figures

Dealing with authority figures can be a real problem for most of us at some time. Bosses, policemen, doctors, teachers, parents - anyone who can wield power over us - might be able, with the raising of an eyebrow, to reduce us to cowering wimps. Naturally we will have to judge each situation on its merits and decide how assertive we are going to be. Sometimes it is in our own interests to pay lip service to the powers that be - it's far better to be slightly deferential and apologetic to a policeman who might otherwise arrest us, for instance - but in most situations, an assertive approach will bring far better results than a cowering one.

So, you have to face up to someone who terrifies you - perhaps your doctor.

The doctor in our scenario is a fearsome individual with a severe expression, disapproving mouth, narrow eyes peering over half-moon glasses, and has a loud and intimidating voice. Each time you see him you become tongue-tied and quivery. You know you are dependent on him for information about your health, but that just adds to your discomfort when you're in the consulting room. How would an assertive person face up to such an ogre?

Read again the four golden rules, do the breathing exercise and then let's go into the doctor's surgery. You've come for a medical which is the pre-requisite for a new job you've been offered. He does the necessary tests, writes things down on a form, but gives you very little information about his findings. You are anxious to know, but reluctant to ask because he seems to be in a bad temper about something.

You need to conquer your fear by rationalising the situation, something like this: "the doctor is there to serve me and look after my health, he has information about me which I would like to know. My feelings and needs are at least as important as his, so it is up to me to let them be known."

Instead of asking for the information meekly and apologetically, you decide to ask for it in a well-modulated tone of voice, which will tell the doctor: I have a right to ask this question and I expect you to answer it.

"What blood count reading did you get, doctor?"

He might reply with a snort: "I'll put it all in my report. Nothing to worry about."

The assertive person would not be put off by the doctor's brusque manner, rationalising that he is not responsible for the doctor's bad temper or sour demeanour, he is only responsible for his own feelings, and they are telling him to ask for information.

So, in the same tone of voice, and without apology, the assertive person will say: "I'd quite like to know the precise reading, could you tell me what it was please?"

The doctor, not used to having his power questioned by mere patients, might try to use some kind of manipulative technique to scare you into silence. Perhaps he looks at you severely down his long nose and says with a patronising sniff: "Why on earth do you want these figures, they won't mean anything to you. Take my word for it, there's nothing to worry about."

At this point the non-assertive man could well give in and apologise for being so pushy. The assertive person, on the other hand, will not have compromised his own stance which says that his feelings are as important as anyone else's and that the information might be useful. He might then say, in the same reasonable and moderate tone of voice: "I know enough about blood measurement to make some kind of sense of the figures. If I need further explanation then I will ask you."

The doctor is blazingly angry by now. "Do you realise how many people I have sitting in the waiting room?" he shouts. "I'm putting all this information in the report as requested. I will advise you if there is anything that needs to be investigated further. Please don't try and tell me my job. I'm a very busy man, so please don't take up my time."

The non-assertive person might now be under the table or fleeing down the street in a flood of tears. The assertive person will, however, be totally unmoved by the doctor's tantrum (on the understanding that each person is responsible for their own feelings), and will simply repeat the request in a measured and moderate way. "I don't wish to question your judgement, I'd simply like the information you've collected about me during your examination. I believe that I am legally entitled to see the report. I don't feel I am being unreasonable."

You are treating your doctor as an equal and demanding that he treats you likewise; any 'authority' that your doctor has rests simply on his greater knowledge of medicine. He does not possess any superior moral authority, nor is he superman. Any image he has of himself as superior is entirely self-created, and only if you accept his assessment of himself can he exercise power over you.

In these days of HIV infection and Aids, more and more gay men are having to deal with the bureaucracy of the health service and with medical practitioners who are either too busy to give full information or too homophobic to treat their gay patients with adequate respect. Once you become part of the hospital system - a "patient" rather than a human being - it is easy to become passive and allow the "experts" to take over. But it is most important that you hang on to your sense of individuality and do not allow health workers to reduce you to a faceless object which has to be processed.

Those who are affected by HIV are in a particularly difficult situation. In many hospitals and treatment centres in the big cities their special needs will be acknowledged and they will be encouraged to take some control of their life and their treatment. It is unlikely that they will meet a medic as monstrous as the one we've just described, but in smaller towns and cities, where the issues are not so familiar, there is likely to be much more ignorance and prejudice. It is in these situations that assertiveness becomes a particularly important tool. If you are going to avoid the sausage-machine syndrome (where you may become a statistic to be 'processed' rather than at real human being with feelings) then you have to let your carers know that you are not prepared to assume the role of helpless, unquestioning victim. You must constantly insist (in an assertive way) that you are part of the decision-making process, that you want to be kept informed of plans that are being made on your behalf. You must take it upon yourself to ask about options, to insist on second opinions where you have doubts about the original suggestion and so on. All this can be done using the techniques suggested in this book, it doesn't have to be done aggressively. An aggressive approach simply alienates those from whom you are seeking help, and that is not the best way to proceed.

Those who are living with HIV and Aids have found that there is a power and a satisfaction in taking control of their own treatment and not simply putting themselves completely in the hands of doctors. Naturally you need their care and expertise, but you also need your own dignity and your own judgement to be respected. For instance, it may be that you have decided that some form of "alternative" treatment might benefit you, but your doctor may be prejudiced against alternative practitioners. He advises you very strongly to steer clear of your homeopath or osteopath or whatever - he thinks they are quacks. Other people have told you that they have benefited from alternative treatment and strongly recommend it. With all the options at your disposal, it is important that you make the decision that is right for you, and that you are not bullied or blackmailed into doing things that you feel are not in your best interests.

Sometimes those living with HIV read widely about their condition and become extremely well-informed, often better-informed than their doctor. Many gay men keep up-to-date with the latest developments and treatments, and occasionally they need to bring these matters to the attention of their medical helpers. Once more, assertiveness can be useful. Some doctors may become alarmed or threatened if they think that their patient knows more than they do about the condition, and so it is important that you gain his or her confidence and respect by behaving assertively from the beginning. That will give you a better relationship when it comes to planning what your best course of action would be in any given circumstance.

To some extent you will be dependent on the medical staff who are treating you, and you will get better treatment if you can impress them with your friendliness as well as your determination. So, don't express your disagreements with them in an aggressive way - do it assertively.

Losing that fear of authority figures may take a lot of practice, but it's worth persevering. Acting the part often helps in this respect; *pretending* to be calm, moderate and reasonable, even though you actually feel like jelly, can be very effective.

If you have problems with people who have authority over you, your anxiety levels will increase when you have to deal with them. If you are in some kind of unpleasant confrontation with them, then the anxiety can become almost unbearable. This is where relaxation can come into its own. Relaxation and anxiety are incompatible and cannot exist in the same individual simultaneously. It follows that if you remain calm and relaxed, you cannot be overwhelmed and conquered by anxiety. Mastering a simple relaxation technique will be most useful if you find that your voice breaks up or you become tongue-tied during these confrontations. If you can prevent your mind becoming a mass of confusion, fear and apprehension, then you will be able to make clear decisions about your behaviour and keep it under firm control. If you know you have to face someone who frightens you, then rationalise the situation beforehand. Try to anticipate how the conversation will go and have your answers and demands ready. Go over the four rules of assertiveness again. Take several deep breaths just before facing the fear-inducing situation and make a conscious effort to slow down. Many actors use variations on this technique to counter stage-fright.

Always be aware of your emotional responses - if you feel you are losing control of your reactions (perhaps becoming unreasonable, petulant, stammering or aggressive) tell yourself that you need to take control, and then do so. By all means tell people that you feel angry or nervous if you feel that it is important for them to know, but don't let those feelings dictate your actions.

And remember what we have said about body language. Standing or sitting up straight, keeping your head up and your eyes focused can give you a lot of confidence. You will be at an advantage if you are aware of - and can control - the body signals that reveal your anxiety (worried look, trembling hands and perhaps a sweaty brow).

Remember to keep eye contact when talking to someone - even if they're saying something to you that you don't like. If you fail to look someone in the eye when you're telling them something, then this can be interpreted as evasiveness. But if you maintain eye contact, you are telling the other person that what you are saying is the truth, or at least an honest feeling. Eye contact can be overdone, though. If you stare unwaveringly into a person's eyes it is a signal of aggression (or being in love with them). The rule of thumb is to balance eye contact with occasional glances away - look at some other part of their face or glance down from time to time.

Don't stand too close to those with whom you are conducting a difficult conversation. Leave about eighteen inches to two feet between you. Standing too close can be intimidating to some people who do not like to have their "personal space" invaded. One again, this rule is turned on its head by people who are in love - they find standing close to each other very pleasant.

If you have a delicate negotiation to complete, try to sit side by side rather than facing each other - this position makes it less confrontational and less likely to get heated.

Bear in mind that you will have some failures as you try these techniques. Don't be put off by a few set-backs, just try to analyse what went wrong, how you could do it better and try not to let it happen again.

Seeing these scenarios written down like this may make it seem simple, but it isn't. Each of these situations needs a great deal of pre-planning and complex decision-making, and when you are feeling nervous it is easy to make the wrong choice, to say the wrong words or betray your anxiety with body language that contradicts what you are saying.

Resistance To Your New Behaviour

When you take the first steps towards becoming assertive, be ready for a few bad reactions from those close to you. They may be used to you being compliant and easily dominated. They may have labelled you as 'easy-going', which might mean that you do whatever is asked of you, never saying 'no' to requests, however unreasonable. They might have discovered that you are easy to bully or are susceptible to emotional blackmail. Once you start recognising that you have been subject to all these negative behaviours, and then do something to change them, you will find resistance from those who have found life easier because you were so pliable. If you suddenly start being assertive with a partner who has grown used to having his own way, or with a parent who is making unreasonable demands, you might find some very hostile reactions. In such cases you should remember the four rules of assertiveness and determine to adhere to them, whatever the pressure from you 'significant others' to return to the old ways.

This was Alistair's experience when he decided to be more assertive with his partner Jamie:

"Jamie and I had a relationship which was going nowhere. He wasn't prepared to compromise on anything and insisted on having his own way all the time. I felt put upon and used. I wasn't a very assertive person and nearly always backed down in arguments. Jamie's needs nearly always took precedence over mine. I love him madly, but wasn't in control of my life - I just didn't take part in the decision-making. A friend of mine suggested I took an assertiveness course, and after I'd been on it, I was able to analyse precisely what it was about Jamie's behaviour - and mine - that was holding me down. He was an ace guilt tripper, and if ever he felt I wasn't going along with his demands he would begin to make it seem as though it was my fault. When I realised what he was doing, I simply called his bluff - in a reasonable, not aggressive, kind of way.

Of course, Jamie didn't like it, he wasn't used to me resisting. He thought I was being unreasonable, he said, and even that I was trying to tell him I wanted to end the relationship. He used every trick in the book get me to behave as I had done in the past - manipulation, emotional blackmail, appealing to my better nature - and when none of that worked, he started getting angry.

I had a feeling that might happen, so when he started shouting I simply walked out of the room without responding. He was completely bewildered by my apparent change of personality, but I didn't think it was fair to use assertiveness as a sort of trick to do him down, so I told him why I had decided to change my behaviour. He didn't like it and vehemently denied that he dominated me, but he's getting used to it bit by bit. He's even started changing his own behaviour, consulting me before doing things that will affect both of us.

It was quite tricky at first, and I was afraid that he wouldn't be able to cope with this new version of me. But I think our relationship is improving. And although he won't admit it, I think Jamie does too. He's coming to see that it's better to have a partner who is equal instead of one who is a compliant child."

There can be no increase in self-esteem until you feel that you are in charge of your own life, and that can't happen until you unapologetically assert your right to be yourself. Given time, your friends, family and colleagues will come to accept this new, more confident you; they might - like Jamie - even come to like you better. Your assertiveness, if practised consistently, will grant them the dignity of equal status, too. Remember, assertiveness is not only about claiming your own rights, it is about granting rights to others. They might find the change hard going, but they'll get used to it.

Finally, there is always a choice as to whether you will be assertive in any given situation. You don't have to be assertive all the time, sometimes it's better just to let things pass. If you judge that the emotional energy required to assert yourself does not merit the potential return, then don't expend it. If you feel that letting someone "win" an argument occasionally will not compromise your dignity or theirs, then you can sometimes choose to let it go. Life would be unbearable if every little disagreement had to be carried through to its just conclusion. Sometimes it's easier and simpler all round just to shrug and say "so what?" This, in it's way is being assertive, too. Sometimes it's pleasurable to be passive and to let other people take care of us for a while.

All these techniques can be applied to day to day life, and if used frequently and in as many situations as possible, will have a profound effect on the way you see yourself. Your self-esteem will increase and your new-found self-respect will give you the confidence to face up to the larger changes you need to make in life. But don't underestimate the effort required to get it right. It is probably better if you try to integrate this new behaviour into your life gradually. Start with simple situations which don't generate much anxiety and you'll have a better chance of succeeding. One success in a relatively minor situation can give you the confidence to try these techniques in other areas of your life.

Sit down now and make a list of the situations which you feel assertiveness could be helpful to you. Grade them in terms of the amount of anxiety each situation generates in you. For example, the list might be: talking to the boss on a social level; initiating conversations with strangers; talking to your parents about your homosexuality; saying no to your partner when he makes unreasonable demands; challenging your work colleagues when they don't pull their weight. Your anxiety rating might be: 'the prospect of talking about homosexuality with my parents makes me unbearably anxious; seeing my boss on a social level makes me quite anxious; initiating conversations with strangers makes me slightly uncomfortable; being dumped on by colleagues at work is irritating.'

It is obvious that if you make your first assertiveness project 'talking to your parents about your homosexuality', the likelihood is that you'll be so full of fear and anxiety that you'll make a real mess of it. Leave that for another time when you're feeling a little more practised and familiar with assertiveness. Start at the bottom of the list.

If your work colleagues regularly give you extra work which is rightfully theirs, then resolve to refuse assertively next time they try it. Read through the techniques again and plan your strategy. Remember to say what you feel and what you want clearly and confidently. Don't get angry, keep your body language under control, and remember the all-important tone of voice. Be reasonable and retain your dignity, and at the same time, allow them to retain theirs. No unwarranted accusations or insult hurling. You're unlikely to get a satisfactory reaction from that approach.

Remember, you don't have to elaborate any further than you want to. Watch out for fogging, and if necessary use the broken record technique to get your point over.

Keep your feelings under constant review during your confrontation, and if you feel they are getting out of control (anger might be rising) then acknowledge them but don't let them lead. If you are likely to get anxious or angry, remember to try the breathing exercise before you begin. If you succeed in your endeavours, chalk up a success and move on to the next situation. If it didn't work, and the situation continues, then sit down and analyse what went wrong and how you might be more effective in subsequent attempts. Best of all, reward yourself for every attempt, whether it is successful or not.

Spontaneity And Anger

It may seem from all this that far from allowing our feelings free expression, we are trying to control them. This is true in one way but not in another. We are trying not to become the victims of our feelings, but to co-exist with them. If you are angry with yourself, then that is your feeling and you are entitled to it. Far better to bang the table and swear or throw a plate at the wall than to try to suppress it and end up with a festering frustration eating away inside you. But when you are angry with other people, then the rules of assertiveness still apply. However foolish you perceive them to have been, they still have their right to dignity. You are allowed to make mistakes and to forgive yourself, and so are other people.

Anger is much misunderstood as an emotion. The expression of anger is thought of by many people in our society as being undesirable or impolite. However furious some people are inside, they wouldn't dream of expressing that "inappropriate" feeling. In assertiveness, anger is a legitimate feeling just like any other. But feeling angry is not the same as being violent or aggressive. You can tell people that you feel angry about something that they have done without having to compromise their rights or dignity. Expressing anger to someone does not mean that you have to beat them up or abuse them verbally. It simply means that you are entitled to tell them how you feel at that time about something they have done or said. The constructive release of angry feelings is desirable. Not only does it stop the feeling festering and creating resentment and anxiety, it also helps the other person confront and deal with whatever they have done to create the anger.

Anger that is expressed constructively does not become an expression of aggression which is intimidating, humiliating or violent for other people.

There are, basically, three types of anger: focused, unfocused and repressed. Let's illustrate all three in action with a little tale of office life. The boss has just had a big row with his M.D. on the phone. He is furious, red in the face, shaking with anger and ready to strangle the first person he sees. Enter Mr Stoop, the office clerk, who has been trying for days to work up the courage to ask the boss for a salary increase. He knocks on the door. "What is it?" bellows the boss. Mr Stoop enters the room tentatively.

"What do you want, Stoop?" growls the boss.

"I...er...wonder if I could have a word with you about..."

"Have you finished this month's stock check yet?" asks the boss, regarding Stoop as a convenient lightning rod through which to discharge his fury.

"Well, no not yet, I just wanted..."

The boss rises from his chair and strides across the room "Get out of my way, Stoop," he bawls, shoving poor Mr Stoop into the corner, where he falls over a wastepaper basket, spilling the contents all over the floor. The boss stomps out and slams the door with such force that a picture falls off the wall. Mr Stoop is now shaking with anger. How dare the boss treat him like that? He has no right to talk to him in such a way.

Enter the boss's secretary. "What on earth have you being saying to the boss, Mr Stoop?" she asks. "He's in a foul mood."

"Oh, I don't think it was anything to do with me, Miss Smith," says Mr Stoop with a weak smile. "He was in a bad mood when I came into the room. I think I'd better get on with my work or I'll be in for a roasting later."

"Oh dear," says Miss Smith, seeing the mess all over the floor. "I expect you realise that I have to keep this office clean, Mr Stoop. When the boss comes back he'll be angry if there's broken glass over the floor and all that screwed up paper. It's very annoying when I have to clean up after other people. I think you really ought to clean up the mess, given it's your fault."

Mr Stoop is left in the room, trembling with a volcanic anger that has no escape route. He picks up the broken picture and the spilled contents of the waste paper bin.

If we go over this scene, we'll see that the boss's anger was real, he had acknowledged it, but it was unfocused and was hurtling all over the place. It wouldn't have mattered really who had been first through the door, the anger would have hit all-comers. We can see the injustice that can easily arise from unfocused anger flying around like a guided missile with a faulty computer. Anger should be directed towards a constructive end or it will never be resolved.

A more focused anger - although it's arguable whether it is correctly focused - was expressed by Miss Smith, who was annoyed that she would be expected to clear up the mess which she perceived was Mr Stoop's fault. Instead of simply suppressing that anger, she expressed it to the person whom she considered was appropriate. This is focused anger, and is what the assertive person would choose. Miss Smith is probably an assertive (and maybe sometimes aggressive) person, who speaks directly. With a bit of fine tuning, she can minimise the aggression and maximise the assertiveness.

Mr Stoop, on the other hand, is anxious not to cause upset or incur any further victimisation, and so he takes the passive stance, keeping his anger bottled up and fuming within. He is angry at the situation and with the way people are treating him, but he is also angry with himself for letting it happen without demur.

Anger is a real emotion, and it needs to be acknowledged and expressed. But choose to focus your anger and, when you are dealing with other people, make it just.

5: ASSERTIVENESS AND COMING OUT

"Stepping back into the closet only increases the level of oppression. And, although I've been accused of being a Pollyanna, I do think things are getting better,"
Armistead Maupin, author "Tales from the City".

Coming out to parents, friends and family can be the most difficult area of all for the insecure homosexual man. But, as we've seen, failure to come out means that our gay life will not progress very far, and staying in the closet will impede the development of our gay self-esteem. If we don't acknowledge and integrate our sexuality into our wider existence, we are denying ourselves the opportunity of a full and fulfilling emotional life. Coming Out is the seminal experience for homosexuals, the key that opens all the other doors to happiness and adjustment. It is also probably the most terrifying thing that many of us can imagine.

Assertiveness will not completely remove the trauma from the coming out experience, but it will significantly increase your chances of success. You will be able to retain your dignity in the face of what might be a gruelling family crisis and also help others to cope better with their feelings about this great event in your lives.

No two families are the same, and so there can be no hard and fast rules. All decisions have to be taken in the light of your own assessment of the situation and of people's receptiveness. You need to think of the time, the place and many other practical considerations. As all relationships are unique, only you can decide how best to approach this topic with your family. You will have to create your own scenario for using assertiveness to help you through the trying times ahead.

Don't Catastrophise

The first thing to remember, though, is that you are master of your own destiny. Re-read the four golden rules of assertiveness and apply them in this situation. If you have decided that the time has come to be open and honest with your parents, face the decision with courage and be prepared for the consequences. Reactions might be bad, but the likelihood is that they won't be. It is important not to *catastrophise* (the favourite occupation of those with low self-esteem). To catastrophise means a tendency to predict and anticipate the most horrendous consequences resulting from every risk taken. ("I couldn't possibly tell my parents, they'd drop dead immediately" or "No, my old friend John wouldn't understand if I told him. He'd never speak to me again.") Catastrophising can provide a great, if frequently spurious, motivation for doing nothing. If things are going to be so bad, why make them worse? But catastrophising is often based on self-delusion and pessimism. There is little - beyond death - that is totally irrecoverable. If we are strong we can recover from the blows that life delivers, and if we are imaginative and persistent we can make something of the setbacks that might befall us. Don't project the worst possible outcome on every decision you are faced with - think positively, and try to see the benefits of making changes.

What's Your Motive?

Next, look carefully at your motivations. Why do you want to come out to your family? One of the answers, hopefully, is that you want to be free from the fear of discovery and so be liberated to live an honest and dignified life. Ideally you will want to take the plunge because you desire your relationships with your loved ones to be more open and less fraught. If these are your reasons, then you should go ahead and make a start.

If your reasons are less noble - for instance, you see your coming out as a means of "getting back" at your parents for some wrong you feel they have done you, then perhaps you had better give the matter some more thought. Using your homosexuality as a weapon to punish parents is not a good basis for making improvements in your life. You cannot come out assertively or with dignity if your principal purpose is to cause pain - such a tactic will surely backfire. If you are unhappy now, this kind of behaviour will simply make things worse. Remember, assertiveness is not about trampling over the feelings of others. It is about granting each other equality.

We must be careful, though, not to fall into the trap of staying in the closet in order to "spare" our parents distress. That is faulty logic, because it may well spare them from pain, but it prolongs your own suffering. If you face the situation with honesty and goodwill, you can all emerge from the other side stronger and closer. It was Margaret Adams who first wrote about the Compassion Trap and it is worth mentioning here. Compassion is, of course, a noble virtue and a facet of human life that makes it worthwhile, but only when it is a genuine expression of empathy with other people and not a means of enslaving yourself to their demands. Sympathising with the pain and suffering of others is quite distinct from allowing it to overwhelm and paralyse you emotionally is something quite different. Reject the argument that you are behaving selfishly by telling your parents you are gay, and therefore causing them unnecessary grief. If you are doing it for the right reasons, then the emotional turmoil which you might have to work through will be justified.

The argument then goes that if you leave things as they are, unspoken and unexplored and dishonest, then everyone can carry on as normal and all this upheaval can be avoided. Although this may be satisfactory from your parents point of view, but it's far from satisfactory from yours. Inflicting upon yourself the burden of lies that goes with staying in the closet can have terrible consequences - some of which we've already discussed. Acting assertively, you know that your feelings and opinions are as important as anyone else's - and that includes your parents, brothers, sisters and friends. So, coming out to them with the best of loving intentions is far better than either staying in the closet and harming yourself or coming out with the primary intention of settling some kind of score.

They might be upset at first, but most people get over it and then get on with life. Keeping in mind your right to choose a full life of your own direction, you should ride out any crisis, maintaining your dignity while giving your parents, family or friends the reassurance and support that they might need. Remember, the discomfort and upset that will probably follow the revelation is a necessary passage to a newer and more mature relationship. It's rather like having to undergo surgery to cure a life threatening illness - the surgery is frightening and unpleasant, maybe even painful, but the end result is a healthier you. You had to endure agony, fear and inconvenience in order to rid yourself of the illness. And so it is with coming out.

So, how do you actually come out assertively?

Much will depend on the circumstances of your life: your age, the kind of relationship which already exists between you and your family and whether you still live with them at their home. If you decide to go ahead, you might find that parents will resist the news at first. What follows are some of the arguments that other gay people have faced from their parents after they came out, and then some of the counter arguments.

♦ You're only doing this to hurt us.

This may well be the way they feel at the time but, as we've already discussed, telling the truth for the right reasons is not meant to hurt but to heal. If you can reassure them that you have done this because you love them and want to be honest with them, most parents will understand, given time. Try to ensure they appreciate the pain you've had to suffer through being dishonest with them, and how your decision to tell will lead to a better relationship. It may take some time for them to accept this reasoning.

♦ It's just a phase, you'll get over it when you meet the right girl.

This argument is often employed by parents as a defence mechanism, a way of pushing aside what is painful. If you are in no doubt about your sexuality then ensure they understand from the start that you don't consider it to be in any way temporary. By calmly but firmly insisting that you don't accept the 'phase' interpretation of events, then you can encourage your parents to face up to the truth much sooner.

♦ **Where did we go wrong, it must be our fault that you're like this.**

Guilt is a frequent reaction to the news that a child is gay. Trying to assume responsibility for your orientation is one way that parents can begin to understand. When they first discover the truth they will be thrashing around for 'reasons' to explain your sexuality. They want an explanation for something which is a mystery. They have probably also heard the theory that male homosexuality is "caused" by a domineering mother or an absent father. This theory originated in the 1960s from a study conducted by Professor Irving Bieber. His study has been repeatedly discredited, and more and more evidence is accumulating which seems to suggest that there is some physical explanation for homosexuality - that there may be a genetic or hormonal element in the way we develop. Nothing is certain, though, and so parents cannot blame themselves for 'causing' you to be gay.

♦ **You'll get Aids, they all do.**

If you aren't already infected by HIV (the virus which is thought to lead to Aids) then there is no reason why you need ever contract it. Despite the messages your parents might have picked up from irresponsible newspapers, Aids and homosexuality are not synonymous. The modes of transmission for this virus are now well understood and safer sex practices can ensure that even the most sexually active gay men can avoid HIV. Reassure your parents that you know this information and that you intend to be responsible and vigilant. Give them some suitable reading material which might help them - my book *A Stranger in the Family - How to Cope If Your Child Is Gay* (The Other Way Press) might be suitable.

If you are, in fact, HIV positive, then coming out to them about your sexuality and your antibody status might be a simultaneous issue. Once again, assertiveness can be helpful. The fact that HIV infection carries with it such a stigma makes everything that much more difficult (and even if you are free of any symptoms, your family are still likely to consider you to be "ill"). In most cases, families have rallied round and been supportive and generous. Many gay men suffering from HIV-related conditions have returned to their parents homes for tender loving care and been received with magnanimity. Make sure you fully understand your condition and that you can explain it comprehensively and authoritatively to them. If they cannot handle the news and they refuse to accept you, then you should seek assistance elsewhere in the gay community. There are many facilities which have been created to take care of those suffering the double burden of HIV infection and social rejection.

♦ **It's against God's law. You ought to pray for forgiveness.**

If you come from a background of strict religious belief, there are extra problems, some of which might be insurmountable. Assertiveness can help you rationalise the situations and resist emotional manipulation. Religion, on the other hand, puts such thinking entirely into reverse, depending as it does on an unquestioning belief in the unseen and the unknown. It means allowing someone else to make your important decisions for you. Strict and dogmatic religious communities can be extremely cruel to those of their members who do not fit into the "pre-ordained" mould.

If religion is important to you, then remember there are choices, even in that area. The Lesbian and Gay Christian Movement has another way of looking at the Bible and there are Jewish gay groups, too, which can help.

However, if you want to come out to parents who subscribe to a philosophy of religious fundamentalism (the literal interpretation of the Bible) it is highly unlikely that they will take the news of your homosexuality with equanimity. One person who has survived such an experience is Jeanette Winterson, the lesbian author of *Oranges Are Not the Only Fruit*. In an interview she described her feelings when, in early life, she reached a turning point that would oblige her to make the choice between her religious upbringing and her burgeoning sexuality: "Everyone reaches a moment when they come to a cross-roads - whether to go on with the life you know, which is safe and comfortable, or move on to another, which is more dangerous and, maybe in the end, unsatisfying. You have to cross over and take the risk or move back and make compromises. In my case it was not possible to belong to an evangelical church and love a woman. And I was also going to a world that was really was not acceptable to many people, or safe." In these circumstances the choice may be as stark as that: move on and take risks or go back and suppress your needs in order to remain true to your religious principles.

It is possible that your family will surprise you and be more accepting than you could have imagined, but the community they live in is unlikely to be as understanding.

♦ We can't understand it, we can't accept it.

The cry that heterosexuals "can't understand" homosexuality is a frequent one. Often they will go as far as to say that they find us repulsive. This might be true *but it is not your responsibility that they feel this way.* They are suffering from homophobia and like every other phobia it is an irrational and morbid condition. You have not created this phobia, you are simply the victim of it. Consequently, you cannot be made to assume responsibility for its existence. If your mother faints at the sight of a spider we need to ask: does the spider have a problem, or does your mother? Psychologists have now discovered that people who suffer from phobias can be quite easily cured with the right treatment. In other words, it is not you who is sick, but they.

Similarly, parents may not understand your feelings simply because they don't share them. But that doesn't mean they can't accept them. Truly mature individuals allow other people to feel differently without getting upset. If your parents become agitated because they "can't understand", try to make them see that they don't have to understand, they just need to accept. If the thought of physical expression of homosexuality "makes them sick", then they simply don't need to think about it. The physical expression of your sexuality is really a personal thing, and it's unlikely that they'll be required to witness it. If you have heterosexual brothers or sisters who are married or in a some other sexual relationship, it is likely that your parents don't really like to think of them in their intimate moments, either. They cope by simply not thinking about it, they just accept that it happens. They should extend the same privilege to you.

Parents - and other people who claim not to understand - simply have to grow up and come to terms with the fact that not everyone in the world feels the same way that they do. Those who are incapable of this leap of imagination and empathy usually end up as bigots - and very unhappy and bitter individuals to boot. Their bigotry is a sad problem, a sign of a pathetic immaturity, and they have to sort it out for themselves. It is your problem only in so far as its effects spill into your life from time to time.

As for their not being able to "accept" your gayness - what does that mean? Of course they could accept it, what is to stop them but their own fear? Some parents have very little problem adjusting to their child's homosexuality; they may not be over the moon about it, and they may have to revise their expectations, but they have accepted. So can your parents. It is no use their saying that because they had a strict and disapproving upbringing they are bound by this. Remind them that they are not responsible for *their* parents' feelings, and they are allowed to think and feel differently. They are permitted to move on. It is not carved in tablets of stone that every generation must hold the same opinion as the one before. If that were true the world would never progress and we'd still be living in caves.

You might be one of the lucky ones who have reasonable, informed and liberal-minded parents. Then again, you may have parents who have inherited and embraced attitudes which make the acceptance of a homosexual son very difficult. During all this ferment, assertiveness will be useful. It won't make you totally immune to bad feelings, but it will help you cope with them. It won't totally prevent pangs of guilt penetrating but it will help you identify them.

For instance, if your parents are trying to blame you for the way they feel ("Why did you have to tell us? If you'd kept quiet we could have carried on as normal and needn't have had all this upset"), then you may well accept their analysis and take on the mantle of guilt they have laid at your door. This will lead to depression and regret. It will undermine your self-esteem and have the opposite effect to the one you had intended. Once you have analysed and rationalised the source of your depression ("They are blaming me for feeling which they themselves have created") you can relieve yourself of the responsibility with a clear conscience. After a lifetime of such guilt trips, you might not find it easy to resist, but you must try. It may be that your parents don't realise precisely what they are doing by off-loading their own guilt and bad feelings on to you.

Prepare well for what might be an extremely uncomfortable time. Hopefully you will have practised assertiveness techniques in other areas of life and will be prepared to try them in the context of your sexuality. Remember:

1. Keep calm. Try to keep anxiety under control by applying relaxation methods.

2. However badly your parents react, don't join in their emotional explosion. If they shout, don't shout back. If they cry, try to stay dry-eyed. Keep your voice quiet, reassuring but confident. Don't be afraid to say how you feel - "I am nervous about your reactions", "I feel sorry that you are having such a bad time," "This isn't easy for me either", "I'm so happy that you are taking it so well" etc. - and listen carefully to what they are saying to you. Constantly remind them why you are coming out and why it is so important to you and to them. If things seem to be getting out of control, ask if you can take some time out - go for a walk, listen to relaxing music, meditate, try your best to relax. Your mind will then be in a better position to weigh the facts and reach a decision about your next move. Creative decisions are much harder to make when you're agitated.

3. Watch out for manipulation. If you've decided to come out to your whole family, don't let your parents persuade you to be selective about who you tell. "Let's just keep it between the three of us" is a familiar tune played by parents to children who have come out. Such a request is seen as a damage limitation exercise, but for you it means keeping the closet door firmly closed in some situations. Explain to them why you can't accept and why you are determined to be out with everyone in the family. Do this calmly, too, refusing to be drawn into the web of guilt your parents might have constructed ("But we are so ashamed, why are you trying to humiliate us in front of the whole family?") An assertive person would see straight through that one. You aren't trying to do anything of the kind to them, you are trying to make things better between you and your family. Their feelings are important, of course, but in the end you have to be true to yourself. Humiliation can only happen if you allow it to happen - they can make the choice to face the family bravely and with head held high. Humiliation would be very difficult in those circumstances.

But, you might say, isn't the rule of assertiveness that other people's feelings must be respected and not trampled under foot? Yes, of course, but let's be clear exactly whose feelings are being trampled here. In this case I believe it is the parents who are running roughshod over the needs and dignity of their gay child. Your parents are not responsible for your feelings, just as you are not responsible for theirs. They don't have to feel ashamed and disappointed, they could just as well choose to feel proud of you. Make sure they realise that they have a choice - rejection is not the only option.

4. Be prepared to explain. This might seem like a contradiction of what we've said before about not having to justify anything you do, and while no-one has an automatic right to an explanation of your actions, in the case of coming out to loved ones, I think it is a good idea to tell them as much as you can about the way things are in your life.

They might react to your news by demanding that you have "treatment" for your homosexuality, or that you see a priest for "forgiveness". If the relationship with your parents is important to you and you want it to continue, you have to be prepared to resist all this with rational and informed argument. Each anti-gay myth to which your parents subscribe will have to be patiently dismantled with logic, each attempt to manipulate you with guilt or emotional blackmail must be recognised and exposed for what it is.

You will have realised by now that the by-word for the assertive person is choice. You always have the option to do something or not to do it, to make a decision or to put it off. Every decision you make will, hopefully, propel you forward towards your goal in life of happiness and fulfilment. Naturally, you can choose to come out or stay in the closet. Sometimes, and in some circumstances, it is right to be circumspect and to make use of the ability to "pass for straight" in order to preserve life and limb. But keeping from those you love the truth about your essential self is a dangerous decision. The cost of avoiding the truth in order to save your 'significant others' from feeling discomfort is a lifetime of denial - and probable psychological damage - for you. The surface waters may remain calm by using the "hiding" choice, but the inner depths will continue to churn.

5. If you need back up, enlist the help of someone your parents can respect. If you are already out to a sympathetic member of the family make sure they will be around to provide a role model for your parents. They can demonstrate best of all that acceptance is a real option. It is amazing what pressure from a sister or brother or uncle or aunt can do to make your parents calm down and reconsider their position. If you haven't come out to anyone in the family, then you could consider getting someone from a gay help line to talk to them, or best of all a member of a parents-of-gays support group. You'll get addresses, phone numbers and other contracts from the listings in *Gay Times* or from Lesbian and Gay Switchboard.

Your parents will have their own "coming out" to face. They will have to decide whom - if anybody - they are going to tell that they are the parents of a gay child. They fear that they will lose prestige in the eyes of their friends, neighbours and work colleagues. They may be afraid that their position in the community will be undermined if it is thought by their friends that they have a "defective" child. However insulted we may be by such a concept, we have to acknowledge that they are real fears for some people, and we have to allow them the time, sometimes years, to sort them out. Parents can't be expected to accept such a fundamental change in their child overnight. They have to reassess a whole swathe of expectations and hopes for the future. They have to deal with a lot of fear and misunderstanding. They need to educate themselves about homosexuality, and what it means for them and you in the years to come. That's a tall order for anyone.

Don't be too impatient and don't be too hard on them. We have to let them experience their feelings. Although we may consider them to be an over-reaction, they are, nonetheless, very real for the people experiencing them. You can allow this adjustment time without having to compromise your own needs.

Let's listen to how Mark came out to his parents, without the benefit of assertiveness.

Mark: Mum, dad, I've got something to tell you, and I hope you won't be too upset about it. I think you may have suspected for some time what it is and I don't want to hurt your feelings. But I do think it is only right that you should know. I'm er...you know...gay.

Mum (*bursting into tears*): Oh no, it can't be true. Tell us it isn't true. Is it a joke?

Mark: No mum, it isn't a joke. I'm really sorry to have to tell you that I really am gay. Sorry.

Dad: It's just a phase. All young people go through it. You'll grow out of it.

Mark: Do you think so? I thought you went through phases when you were a teenager. I'm thirty-two. I don't think it can be a phase, do you?

Mum: How are we going to face the neighbours? What will your grandma say? If she ever finds out it will kill her. You aren't going to tell her are you? Let's keep it to ourselves - after all, there's nothing to be gained by telling other people, is there?

Mark: Oh - OK mum, if that's what you want.

Dad: I don't know why you want to tell anyone. Why do you think we're interested in your sex life? We don't tell you about ours, do we? It's very selfish and arrogant of you to upset your mother like this. I don't understand it at all.

Mark: Sorry dad.

Mum: It's all our fault. Where did we go wrong? We must have done something in his childhood to make him turn out like this.

Mark: I'm really sorry you're upset mum. I wish I hadn't said anything now.

Dad: Well, it's too late now, the cat's out of the bag. I think it would be best if you didn't say any more. You can see your mother's heartbroken, and I'm deeply disappointed in you. I don't want to hear another thing about it.

Mark: But dad...

Mum: Your father's right. It's better if we just forget what you've just said. I don't believe it anyway. You've made a mistake.

Mark: But I wanted to tell you about my life, to be honest with you.

Dad: We know as much about your life as we want to. Why do you have to keep ramming this homosexuality down our throats?

Mark: But I'm not...

Dad: Talking about it all the time.

Mark: But I've never mentioned it before.

Mum: It's so upsetting, going on and on about it. I'll never sleep again, I know I won't. Promise me that you won't do anything...anything unnatural, Mark. (She bursts into tears again).

Mark: I won't do anything silly, mum.

Mum: I can't bear to think about it. You won't go with any men, will you? If you do, I'll kill myself. I won't be able to live with the shame.

Mark: Don't talk like that, mum. It isn't the end of the world.

Mum: It's the end of my world.

Dad: You ought to get treatment.

Poor old Mark. His parents were employing the same sort of tactics which they've probably used on him a million times before. First they denied the truth ("Don't talk about it, we don't want to know") and then they piled on the emotional pressure to try and curtail his further coming out. They didn't want him to explore his sexuality and they wanted him to place his feelings in second place to theirs (which has probably been the scheme of things since he was born). There was little consideration for Mark's needs, even from Mark himself. In effect, they were saying that he should deny himself the possibility of enjoying love and companionship, because it would make them feel uneasy.

These initial reactions, thoughtless and panic-stricken though they are, aren't necessarily the feelings that will prevail if Mark persists. There are several options available for Mark's next move, but at present he has to acknowledge that his parents are in a state of shock and he has to allow them time to recover. There's not much point in telling them they are being irrational, selfish, illogical and manipulating - they are in no fit state to hear that. After a few days, or maybe a few weeks - however long it takes the dust to settle - Mark can move to the next phase. But let's run that coming out scene again, this time applying an element of assertiveness to the episode.

Assertively Gay

Mark: Mum, dad, there's something I want to tell you. I've been meaning to get round to it for some time. I'm gay. I know it might shock you, but I hope you'll try to understand.

Mum: You're joking. It's a joke isn't it?

Mark (*in a reassuring and calm tone of voice*): No, it's not a joke. I'm very serious, and it's taking all my courage to tell you this.

Dad; It's a phase - all young people go through it. You'll grow out of it.

Mark: No, dad, it isn't a phase. I'm thirty-two and I've known for a long time that this is how I feel. I just didn't know how to tell you.

Mum: I'm so ashamed. I don't know how I'll face the neighbours.

Mark: I'm sorry you feel like that, mum, because I don't see this as something to be ashamed of. But I understand your feelings. I hope you'll see it differently eventually.

Dad: Why did you have to tell us, anyway? We don't tell you about our sex life, why do you have to tell us about yours. It's very selfish of you to upset your mother like this.

Mark: I think it's a very important issue, and it's about more than just sex. It's about my whole life and where it's going. I wanted to tell you because I think it's time we were honest with each other. I don't want mother to be upset, and I hope she'll soon feel better about it.

Mum: I'm devastated. I shall never sleep again. I'm sure we did something terrible in your childhood to make you turn out like this.

Mark: There's nothing you could have done to make it different, mum. Nobody knows why some people are gay and others aren't. You shouldn't blame yourself. I know what a shock it has been, but I think you'll feel differently when you've had time to think about it. I didn't want to keep on telling you lies, that's all. You must have been wondering why I wasn't married, and where I spent my time and who with.

Mum: I can't stand the shame of it. What will your grandma think? She'll die if you tell her. You know how fond of you she is.

Mark: I'm very fond of her, too. I think she will be understanding. I can talk to her openly about most things, and she doesn't seem to be easily shocked. I want to be honest with her, too, because she is important to me.

Mum: I'm going to commit suicide.

Mark: I'm very sorry that you feel that way, mum, but I can't make it any different. I hope that you'll allow some time for us to try and work it out. I don't think things are going to be as bad as you think they're going to be. If you'd like to talk to someone who knows what it feels like, I have the telephone number of a counselling service run by other mothers who have gay children. They might be able to help you.

Dad: I think it's best if we leave the matter alone. We don't want to talk about it any more.

Mark: I'm sorry dad, but it's taken me a long time to pluck up the courage to tell you this, and I don't want to let all that worry go to waste. I hope that when you've had time to think about it, and have calmed down a bit, we can talk about it again. It's not something that will simply cease to exist because you don't talk about it. I don't want you to be any more upset, but now the news is out, we might as well try to make the best of it, and that means facing up to it fair and square. I love you both very dearly, and I want us to be able to conduct out lives honestly. If you want to ask any questions, please do - anything you like. Call me whenever you want and come round to the flat if you feel like it. You're always welcome. I promise you that this isn't the end of the world - I'm the same person who was here yesterday.

Mark refused to be manipulated by mother's histrionics - although he did acknowledge that her feelings were real. He was sensitive to their panic, but not the victim of it. He kept his voice well-modulated, calm and reassuring. He refused to let their fear and apprehension dictate the direction of the conversation. He knew what he had to say, and he made sure he said it - as many times as was necessary to make them understand that he meant it. The whole thing could have escalated into a full-scale disaster if he had followed their lead with counter-accusations, further attempts at manipulation and an even louder voice.

Most of the parents I have spoken to who have been through this crisis have eventually come to terms with the fact that they have a gay son. When they reach this stage, it will be up to you to move them along. Don't allow them to stick at the point of grudging acceptance or refusal to talk about it. Your own persistence, dignity and understanding of their feelings, will help you all to pass on to complete acceptance and a new dawn of understanding.

If, after persistent efforts, your parents refuse under any circumstances to even try and understand what you are saying to them, then you should seek support elsewhere. The time may have arrived for you to move out into the world on your own, in order to be able to take control of your life. Of course, it would be better if there could be a mutual respect and tolerance, but if that is not possible, it should not deter you from seeking your own fulfilment.

6: GAINING CONFIDENCE

A lack of self-esteem can manifest itself in different ways. As we've seen some people are aggressive and domineering, others are over-achievers; some are passive doormats at the beck and call of everyone while others are charmers who will do almost anything to avoid disapproval.

Another manifestation of damaged self-esteem is shyness. Those who lack a good opinion of themselves may withdraw as much as possible from contact with others. They may become anti-social to the point that they lose the ability to make any effective human relationships. Shyness may seem cute in some people, but in fact it can be a crippling barrier to leading an effective and fulfilled life.

Hurt by a history of humiliation and aggression, some gay men have sometimes subconsciously chosen to opt out of as much as they can of life's rough and tumble. They have stopped taking risks because they are afraid of experiencing even more humiliation.

Those people who lack social skills will often look on with envy at others who seem able to make conversation effortlessly, and who face challenges with enthusiasm rather than dread. They sigh when they see these apparently super-confident individuals looking totally at home in any situation and in any company. "Lucky things!" the socially inept and shy person will say. "It must be wonderful to be so easy-going. Some people are just born charmers."

What they fail to understand is that confidence and social poise are learned behaviours. Nobody is automatically charming and engaging, they have to work at it. The only luck involved is that those who seem to flow through life brimming with confidence have probably had good teachers.

We should differentiate here between those who use charm and humour as a means of avoiding confrontation, and those who are true to themselves and *still* remain attractive. Those who cover their lack of confidence and self-regard with a show of smiles, acquiescence and empty flattery are often very passive individuals who are trying hard not to commit themselves to anything. After all, someone might not approve of what they say and that, in the eyes of the non-assertive, would be the equivalent of total condemnation. So fragile is their sense of self-esteem that they will go to any length - even to the extent of supporting the vilest and most bigoted opinions - in order to deflect criticism from themselves. They would not take the risk of challenging anyone's stance on anything, lest the fury be turned on them, thereby exposing what they perceive to be their worthlessness.

The shy individual has much in common with the empty charmer. Both have compromised their own needs and feelings in order not to risk further damage to their self-regard. Of course, not everyone is so chronically shy that they are completely incapable of human interaction, but most of us suffer from shyness to some extent. A survey by a women's magazine showed that as many as 72 per cent of respondents considered themselves to be shy to some extent and in some situations.

For most of us shyness means little more than the occasional feeling of discomfort when, perhaps, meeting new people or accepting a challenge. But for others it can be a real disability, greatly restricting the enjoyment of life.

Assertively Gay

Shyness and lack of social skills are not problems for homosexual people alone, but some gay men are made shy by unhappiness with their sexuality. They avoid social situations because they are afraid that their secret will be discovered and it will lead them into rejection or humiliation. Usually such people have had a string of bad experiences - sometimes going back many years - which may have shattered their confidence and increased their unwillingness to stray far from their usual routine and familiar surroundings. So low is their self-esteem that for shy people, rejection on any level can be soul-destroying. The motivating factor in their life becomes: how do I avoid such painful rejection? The answer seems obvious - don't put yourself into any situation where it might occur. Keeping people at a distance will also minimise the risk. The result is loneliness and depression and an ever-decreasing ability to make social contacts that could improve the quality of life. Shy people are caught in a trap from which it is very difficult to escape, but with a large effort and a lot of determination, escape *is* possible. Using assertiveness and other techniques, the gay man who is almost reclusive because of low self-esteem, can overcome fear and become a fully-functioning member of society.

Here is a list of what needs to be done:

1. Make a pact with yourself that you are going to change your life for the better.

2. Get to like yourself and increase your sense of self-worth.

3. Overcome your fear of your sexuality.

4. Learn to use effective social skills.

A tall order indeed, but one to which you should give serious thought.

You've already read in earlier chapters about how gay people can become separated from their essential selves and how coming out can be a catharsis that makes them whole again. Now it is time for you to face up to your own sense of self-alienation. It is time to look your long-denied sexuality in the face and say: "I can get to like you, let's make a go of it." You can demolish the emotional Berlin wall that has been keeping you from your true feelings.

One cardinal rule which may seem obvious, but still needs to be stated, goes like this: *you can't be loved by everyone.* For all its obviousness there are an amazing number of gay people who really try to live life under the assumption that they *can* be loved by everyone. They will go to any lengths in order not to upset people. They will ruthlessly compromise and dismiss their own needs so as to make a good impression, to elicit a smile or to be thought well of. Their chief ambition is to be regarded as "nice". The more you are liked, they reason, the less likely people are to challenge you about your homosexuality. The problem with this thinking is that you have to sacrifice important parts of your personality on the altar of other people's feelings.

If you've ever felt that awful withering sensation when someone draws attention to your sexuality in a negative way, then it is likely that you are uncomfortable being gay. You are afraid of being mocked and consequently become afraid of your sexuality. If you loved yourself, every aspect of yourself - including your sexuality - then such insults would be meaningless.

Remember, for everyone who tries to insult you because you're gay, there will be many others who will be able to see beyond the surface and recognise and admire the good and positive aspects of your personality. Some people will love you and these are the people you should seek out for friendship. But before they can like you, you have to like yourself. Start working on it and don't be put off by boors and bigots, they have no place in your life; their opinions should become irrelevant to you.

So let's say it again: *you can't be loved by everyone*. Embrace that idea and believe it. Once you've internalised it, you've taken a major step forward.

Although it might seem like a trite exercise, try writing down a list of good things you know about yourself. It's an exercise that can help you realise just how much you have going for yourself. Don't be modest when making your list and don't undersell yourself - remember, this is an exercise about giving yourself positive strokes. Flatter yourself, compliment yourself, wallow in the glow of self-regard.

Do you have an interesting eye colour? Beautiful hair? A good sense of dress and style or a well-developed body? Are you becoming stronger by trying to be assertive? Keep your list positive and don't overlook the more abstract qualities. For instance, are you considerate, honest, funny, understanding, courageous? After you've made your list of positive qualities you can begin to catalogue your achievements: how well are you doing at work? What about your hobbies? What skills do you have that others envy? Do you grow better pot plants than anyone else, for instance or are you a good lover? Do people enjoy your cooking? Do you play a musical instrument, or dance better than your friends? Do you have a good singing voice? Don't underestimate anything you can do, even if it's only making a good spaghetti bolognese. It's so important that you know these things about yourself - in a concrete way, not just as a passing thought - that I'm going to ask you to put the book down now and get out your pen and paper. Writing down your list will make it real, will give it a substance that reinforces it in your mind.

Accepting Compliments

Most people with low self-esteem don't recognise compliments when they are offered. "You're such a talented artist", someone might say after seeing a water-colour painted by a shy person. "Oh, it's nothing", says the person with low self-esteem, "a child could have done it". And this is not false modesty, it is a genuine belief that he could not possibly have created anything worthwhile. Such a person will have great trouble making a list of good things about himself, simply because he doesn't believe there are any. But don't give up your task until you've listed at least a dozen good things about yourself - and if you can make it twenty or more, so much the better.

Make a resolution now to listen out for, identify and accept compliments. If someone says you've done a good job or that you have a particularly admirable trait, then thank them and give yourself a pat on the back. Try hard not to dismiss it with a self-inflicted put down ("There's nothing to it really, it's just a knack.")

Even if other people don't yet recognise your talent and virtues, you can recognise them yourself. It takes a bit of courage to do this in the face of the odds, but all the best achievements happened this way. We've all heard how famous composers were mortified to hear their music being booed and criticised at the first performance, and then for that same music to be recognised and loved by later generations. We've heard of inventors who were ridiculed because of ideas that later went on to change the world. These people had to have faith in themselves in the face of disapproval and discouragement. They had to have the courage of their convictions and so do you.

If you've done a good job, and no-one seems to notice, give yourself a reward. Next time you come up against someone whose criticism makes you feel depressed and worthless, think back to some compliments you've had and let the warm glow from them push the negative feedback out of your mind.

Shy people, and others with low self-esteem, frequently neglect their health. It is the ultimate expression of self-contempt. Is this the case with you? Are you over-weight, smoking too much, drinking too much, constantly bothered by minor ailments? Are you always exhausted and unmotivated? Or are you simply unconcerned about your appearance?

Make it another resolution to treat your body better. A new diet, healthier food (and fewer binges), more exercise, less cigarettes and booze or whatever it will take to make you feel more positive about your health. It is highly unlikely that you'll be able to feel more positive about yourself if you are unfit and self-neglecting; a sick body will open the way to a sick mind. So work out a new regime for yourself, starting today. It doesn't have to be anything impossibly demanding - you don't have to start getting up at six o'clock in the morning to go jogging or rush down to the local health centre to take up weight training - just a little extra walking or the occasional swim can make all the difference. It has been medically proven that movement has an effect upon depression. If you are down in the dumps and feeling sorry for yourself, get moving. Walk - even if it's only down to the shop for some wholemeal bread and fresh vegetables. Dance - bop till you drop at the local disco (drinking fruit juice and mineral water instead of alcohol). Not only will you feel better for the exercise, you will also be putting yourself into situations where you can practise your social skills.

Accepting Criticism And Rejection

A lack of self-esteem usually goes hand-in-hand with an over-reaction to criticism. The person who undervalues himself will allow criticism to penetrate into his deepest depths. Even mild criticism can be interpreted as complete rejection. If criticism affects you in this way there are several methods of dealing with it so that it doesn't overwhelm you.

Given that human beings are less than perfect, they will, from time to time, make mistakes. If another human being points out these mistakes, then that is criticism. We need to understand that there are two kinds of criticism: the justified, and the put-down.

Justifiable criticism might come in the form of a telling off from your boss ("You really will have to be more careful with these statistics, this is the second time you've messed them up this week.") or maybe from a friend ("I've been waiting here in the cold for an hour, and I'm very angry that you're so late."). For people with low self-esteem, criticisms such as these are seen as attacks on their very right to exist; they wither and shrink and worry about it for days on end. They are consumed by guilt or churned up by unexpressed anger. Because someone has pointed out a small error, people with low self-esteem may feel that they've been written off completely. If mistakes are made, then criticism is justifiable - most people will accept the criticism and do something about it.

People with low self-esteem, though, will react in other ways, either by trying to deny the error and making up excuses or justifications, or by trying to turn it on the person who is doing the criticising ("Oh, I suppose you're never late? You know I'm always running behind schedule, there was no need for you to get here so early.")

Sometimes a person with low self-esteem will withdraw from the situation after being criticised and vow never to speak to the critic again. In that case, they have taken a perfectly justifiable criticism of some incident and made it into an unforgivable condemnation of their whole being. The reasoning behind such a stance goes like this: "Because John says I have poor dress sense, it's his way of saying he hates me and considers me stupid and tasteless. He's laughing at me."

Maybe the comment from John *was* meant as a put-down rather than an honest statement of opinion, but only you can judge that. If he gets his kicks from trying to humiliate his friends, then you can disregard his criticism. If, on the other hand, he is a good friend who only wants the best for you, then you should listen to what he has to say; and what he is saying is simply that you have a poor sense of dress - not that you are a completely worthless person. He was offering constructive criticism which, to an assertive person, is a valuable thing.

The way to cope in these circumstances (once you've decided that the criticism is justifiable and not a put-down) is to thank your critic for pointing out your mistake and saying that you'll resolve to do something about it. This will not be easy for someone with low self-esteem. Such a person will have noted every little bit of criticism he has ever had all throughout his life and used it to bolster his own low opinion of himself. It's time to stop doing that and to start accepting criticism at face value.

The same principle applies to rejection. Maybe you refuse to take risks because you're terrified of being rejected. You don't risk initiating conversations in case the person you'd like to talk to doesn't respond. You don't go to parties or social gatherings because you know you'll be expected to make small talk - and you're hopeless at it. If you do manage to go to a party, you sit in a corner, huddled up and defensive, unable to start a conversation and not welcoming other people's initiatives.

For some gay people who aren't at ease with their sexuality there may be a fear that when they meet new people (particularly non-gay people) they'll be recognised instantly as gay and rejected or mocked because of it. This was certainly the case with Roger, who seldom socialised away from the gay scene:

"I know that I'm effeminate, I don't have any illusions about it - a lot of people have told me so and continue to tell me so. However, I wasn't aware of my mannerisms until I was about twelve and then at school they started calling me sissy and nancy because of the way I walked and talked. I had no idea how I looked until I saw a video of myself in the school play. I was horrified. I was supposed to be playing Julius Caesar, but it was more like Margot Fonteyn in Swan Lake - all wrists and flowing movements. And my voice! Lisping isn't in it. I realised I was really effeminate and why my classmates called me these names. Up until then, my image of myself had been just like any other little boy - I never thought I stood out from a crowd in the way I do.

I was terribly depressed for ages and became self-conscious about speaking. I hardly uttered a word for days on end and withdrew. After a while I became obsessed with the idea that people could identify me as gay in the street and that they were whispering about me. A real persecution complex, it was. I had all the problems of being an isolated gay person and all the hassle about being effeminate as well. It was terrible. I'm sure my parents thought I was becoming mentally ill, and I think maybe I was. I was so depressed about everything. It went on well after I'd left school, but I couldn't hide for ever and I had to get a job. I started work in a big office and some of the other juniors there gave me the same treatment that I got at school. But I also found that the women who worked in this office were far more accepting and that I got on much better with them than I did with the other men. In fact I made some very deep and happy friendships with women, and hardly any with men. Isn't that strange, given that I'm supposed to be man-mad? Of course, none of these friendships were romantic, it was just that I had more in common with the girls in the office than with the boys. That relieved the loneliness a little bit, but I was still dreadfully shy and avoided new situations where people might realise I was gay and give me a bad name because of it.

After I found my way on to the gay scene, I realised that this was a place I could relax and be myself without being laughed at. That helped me gain a bit of confidence, but I still felt vulnerable once I was back in the straight world. Much as I would have liked to, I couldn't live in the gay world for twenty-four hours a day.

As I got more and more pissed off with this shyness in straight company, I realised that most of it had to do with my being gay. As my self-knowledge increased I realised that my effeminacy was only one aspect of the problem. I hadn't come to terms with being gay at all. I didn't want to be gay because it was such a grief to me, or that's how I saw it at the time. I realise now that it wasn't my gayness that was the problem, but other people's reactions to it. I didn't have the option of passing for straight, because however hard I tried, I couldn't be butch. Underneath it all I still felt everyone thought of me as a nelly queen. If I let my attention slip for one moment while trying to put over this bland, straight image of myself, I realised I was coming across as camp again. In the end, I just had to accept it - I am camp. I don't do it on purpose, it isn't an affectation - as I said, I wasn't even aware of it until I saw that video. It took a long time to get there, but I've accepted that I'm effeminate and there's very little I can do about it. I have stopped allowing other people's reactions to affect me in any way. I've turned into a tough old queen through all these years of resistance, but I hope I haven't become bitter and twisted with it. I've seen so many other femmes become really quite monstrous and disillusioned with life. They are not nice to be around, and I'm not going to end up like that. I have some lovely friends - gay and straight - a nice job which I do well, and I'm on the lookout for a lover. I know I'll find the right person one day because I'm such a loving sort of guy. Someone's bound to snap me up eventually."

Roger's experience is a common one, and many gay men who are considered 'effeminate' have had similar problems. There are two ways that obviously gay men react to the kind of pressures they have to endure, either by becoming defiant and making effeminacy the dominating part of his character, or becoming shy, withdrawn and isolated, avoiding situations in which he fears he might be humiliated.

If you frequent the commercial gay scene you will see many examples of the first reaction. There is no shortage of 'screaming queens' camping it up, being outrageous, cross-dressing and generally giving full expression to all the things of which they are accused. In the safety of the gay pub or club such behaviour is great fun, a release and an affirmation. It isn't so easy to be defiant when you're on your own in the big, wide, hostile world outside.

Many effeminate gay men find an outlet for the larger-than-life personas they have invented for themselves in the field of entertainment. Camp comedians and drag artists are perennially popular. Julian Clary was first seen as an entertainer on the gay circuit, now he appears regularly on television doing the same kind of camp act. He has told in interviews of his school days, when his obviously effeminacy brought much hostility from both his classmates and his teachers. Eventually he made his overtly gay characteristics into a flag of defiance which he waved in the face of the monks who had been charged with his education. By being defiant, Julian Clary had to create some kind of defence for himself: he found that if he could make people laugh, it tended to disarm their violent intentions. Consequently he developed a witty and outrageous way of dealing with disapproval. It has served him well in his chosen career and, best of all, he has been true to himself and his sexuality - he is not one of those camp comedians who make a living out of parodying homosexuality and then denying that they, too, are gay. In the past such comics have been at best ambivalent about their gayness and at worst have denied it in order not to risk what they imagine is the approval of their public.

Quentin Crisp is another famous example of an effeminate man who decided that at an early age he would put two fingers up to world and become "a stately homo of England". He did this in the 1940s when homosexuality was completely outlawed and social condemnation almost universal. To make sure no-one had any doubts about the statement he was making, Mr Crisp dyed his hair a dramatic red, wore make up and flamboyant clothes and made no effort at all to stiffen his wrists or deepen his voice. From reading his autobiography "The Naked Civil Servant", it cannot be said that Quentin Crisp ever had a satisfactory emotional life. Despite all his defiance and refusal to be untruthful, he never managed to find his ideal "tall, dark man" and eventually gave up even looking for him. His effeminacy took away the option, that many of us have, of "passing for straight". It meant that if he was to have a life with meaning for him, he would have to embrace his campness and let it become his *raison d'être*. In his heart, though, it is clear that Quentin Crisp resented his homosexuality. Despite the fact that it made him famous throughout the world, it is clear that he blames it for having limited his life in so many ways.

Quentin Crisp was a child of his time and we can only speculate what course his life might have taken had he been born a couple of generations later; his dyed hair and make up would hardly raise an eyebrow on the streets of London today.

If you consider yourself effeminate, there is no reason why you should have to follow Mr Crisp's example. You don't have to play the part of the extravagant grotesque - unless you want to. If you hanker for a career in the theatre, then by all means pursue it, but if you happen to want to be a diver on an oil rig - or an ambulance driver or a civil engineer - then don't let other people's perceptions of your abilities, based on your body language and speech patterns, hold you back. You might have to work at it harder than most people, but that's a pretty good spur.

People will try constantly to put you into a pigeon-hole. He's a screaming queen, they'll say, and by definition he is witty, bitchy, entertaining and inconsequential - invite him to a party, he's always good for a laugh.

You have the power to resist the pigeon hole, you can refuse to fit the stereotype which has been created for you by someone else. Strong prejudices exist against obviously gay men and the temptation is always there to play up the stereotype as a means of surviving with minimum hassle. In the old days (less than a decade ago) there was little choice. Now there *is* a choice. With a little determination, stereotypes can be resisted and overcome. Remember: you are not doomed to a life of theatrical exaggeration if you don't want it, and there are other ways to cope with bigots other than by retiring from life. There are enough people in the world who will be prepared to look beyond the surface and see you for what you really are. Going with your inner needs rather than your surface appearance is not the easy option, but it certainly the most satisfying.

For every screaming queen who "flaunts it" there are must be ten other effeminate gay men who have chosen the alternative of isolation. Such people keep their interaction with their fellow human beings to an absolute minimum.

In the next few pages, I'm going to tell you about the research I've been doing into the ways human beings socialise. Together, we'll find out how to use this information in our day to day lives to make friendship-forming and socialising easier.

7: THE LONELINESS TRAP

Recently I spoke to a volunteer on the London Lesbian and Gay Switchboard. He told me that the calls he dreads most are the ones about loneliness, and the reduced ability that some people have to make friends. He said:

> "I usually feel I can help in some way with calls about sexual difficulties, relationship problems or discrimination, but when people ring up to say that they just don't seem to be able to connect with others, I'm lost for suggestions. It seems inadequate just to say: keep on trying. Often callers will have been out on the gay scene, finding themselves a corner in a pub or club and standing there all night hoping that something would happen. They didn't talk to anyone the whole evening and no-one talked to them. They would come away feeling worse than ever, convinced that the gay life was shallow, unfriendly and closed to them."

Often newcomers to the gay scene will be struggling to make a breakthrough, to feel easy with themselves and with the milieu in which they long to find a place. They want to find lovers, yes, but often, just as badly, they want a circle of friends with whom they can share the experience of being gay.

Most newly-emerging gay people, finding their way into the gay community for the first time, come to the daunting realisation that they are going to have to start constructing their social life completely from scratch. They may have spent many years before they "came out" socialising exclusively with heterosexuals. While many of the friendships they made might have been important and supportive, gay relationships will have an extra dimension and appeal. Here is how Howard expressed it:

> "I didn't really come out until I was twenty-nine. Up until then I had not sought out any gay friends, and had existed in the sort of social milieu that was expected of me: I went to the cricket club, the working men's club, the straight discos and so on. Most of the people I counted as friends I had known since I was at school. I'm sure some of them must have also have been gay - or at least have had gay feelings - but I never broached the subject with anyone. I was too scared that it might backfire. I thought having these friends was OK, and I got on with most of them very well, but in the end I simply had to do something about finding other gay people. I was reading about the gay scene in magazines and seeing programmes on the television. I knew my life was passing me by, and if I didn't make an effort it would be too late. So I found my way to the local gay pub. It was only when I was standing in there, clutching my drink in front of me like a protective shield, that I realised that I didn't know a single soul in this new world, and I was going to have to start again at the

age of twenty-nine. That was an appalling prospect. Not that I've ever had trouble making friends, it's just that friendship has always sprung up in my life quite spontaneously from circumstances. You know: at work, at the cricket club and so on. It seemed strange having to go out with the specific intention of 'making friends'. It seemed artificial and doomed to failure, but at the same time, I knew that if I didn't do it, I wasn't going to make myself the life that I wanted.

The gay scene can be an awe-inspiring place, too. Wherever I went everyone seemed to know each other and that made me feel even more like an outsider who was intruding. How on earth are you supposed to get to know people when they seem so intimately involved with one another?"

It didn't take Howard long to realise that most of the people in those bars were there in the hope of finding someone to have sex with. Although each small group of friends seemed self-contained and impregnable at first sight, Howard knew almost instinctively how to signal to people that he was interested. He felt that he was reasonably attractive, and it became clear that a lot of other people agreed with him. Soon he was confident enough to make eye contact with individuals he liked the look of, and to offer a drink if they responded. A gay bar has its own etiquette, and striking up conversations with strangers is the done thing - and generally welcome if both parties find each other attractive. If people don't want to talk to you, they'll soon let you know.

For other people the commercial gay scene can appear unfriendly and even hostile, particularly in London. This is how Dennis put it:

"Even now, after many years socialising in gay circles, I still get the impression when I'm in a gay pub or club that everyone is having a better time than I am. I always feel uncomfortable or nervous, whereas everyone else seems to be brimming with confidence and having the time of their lives. I know this isn't true and that others are lonely, too. But I often feel as though there is something wrong with me because I frequently feel isolated and shut out from all the merrymaking. And while I don't want to give the impression that I am against sex - believe me, I love it - I have to say that in quite a lot of the pubs, the heavy cruising and picking up really puts me off. You feel threatened by all these people looking worried because they haven't managed to score. It's very difficult to have a relaxed time when everyone seems so panic-stricken at the thought that they might not notch up another conquest on their bed post that night."

Those who can function well on the pub and club scene may want to pass on to the next chapter. If starting and sustaining conversations is no problem for you, then you will be well on your way to establishing a circle of friends. If you are easy-going and extrovert when pubbing and clubbing, you're probably already quite well connected. Getting to know only one person can soon lead you on to meeting others.

However, for those whose social skills have become rusty through under-use, it may be necessary to learn to use them all over again. There are other people have never really mastered the art of social interaction and as a result feel lonely and isolated from life. Breaking out of the loneliness trap can be very difficult indeed, and if low self-esteem is the cause of the isolation, then it is even harder.

What Are Social Skills?

What is the purpose of 'social skills' and how do they influence our lives?

Look at this list of statements. Do you ever describe yourself in any of these ways - or variations of them? If you do, then it is likely that one or more of your social skills is rusty and could do with polishing:

"I find it difficult to make small talk."

"I don't think I have any real, close friends."

"I feel there is a barrier between me and other people."

"Sometimes I get the feeling of not belonging, of being an outsider."

"I worry that people will think about me when they find out who I really am, so I keep them at a distance."

"I find it difficult to initiate conversations, I always wait for someone else to make the first move."

"Other people refer to me as quiet or shy."

"I think of myself as quiet or shy."

"I hate the thought of rejection. It makes me feel worthless."

"I couldn't walk into a room full of strangers on my own."

"I think people find me boring."

"Something about me drives people away. My friendships never last."

"I like to stick with the people I know."

"I don't like new situations. I like routine."

"Sometimes I feel alone in a crowd. Parties make me feel terrible."

Nearly everyone feels these things at some time in their lives and young people in particular can find them most distressing. It is not unusual for teenagers and young people to feel depressed, isolated and confused, but for gay people these feelings can be intensified and prolonged well beyond adolescence. Young gays who are experiencing feelings of being 'different' can begin to withdraw quite dramatically. As their friends start to show an interest in the opposite sex, gay youngsters can feel excluded from the peer group. Unless they are lucky, and manage to find some other gay young people who can reassure them and with whom they can share their feelings, it is likely that their gay self-esteem will plummet and their ability to make satisfying friendships might be impaired. The deep sense of confusion about having a sexuality which seems to be universally despised can be devastating for young adults, and can have long-term effects on the way they function in the world. These inhibitions may last well into adulthood, and what little research has been done seems to indicate that gay people start out on their truly independent emotional lives at a much later time, on average, than heterosexuals do.

Deeply internalised doubts about their value can cause some gay men to invent a mythology about the kind of person they are. They apply destructive labels to themselves which become self-fulfilling: "I'm shy" or "I'm boring" or "I'm hopeless at making friends". If you have convinced yourself that you are any of these things, or a thousand other variations on the same theme, then it's time to recognise what you've done and discard the myths. Few are 'naturally' shy or quiet. Look at any group of toddlers and you will be hard-pressed to find one that could be called shy or retiring; maybe children are awkward with strangers at first, but they quickly get over this initial reserve and start bouncing all over their new-found friend, anxious to tell all about themselves.

Young children have few inhibitions - they say what they like, they express their feelings easily and they are naturally curious about the people around them. As they grow up, though, a million negative influences can dampen that charming spontaneity and cause individuals to become shy and reserved. Bad experiences either at home with careless parents or at school from cruel classmates or teachers can destroy a sensitive child's self-esteem and damage him for life. This is particularly true of some gay people who are mortified at being pointed out as 'different' and become withdrawn and isolated as a result.

If you feel you are missing out on life because you are shy or lacking in self-confidence, then there are a few simple techniques which can make that breaking out from isolation a little easier.

Much research has been done into the way human relationships develop. The findings from these studies will seem, to most people, like simple common sense. There are no great revelations or wonderful secrets that will make you popular and well-liked overnight. In fact, the majority of people will have already discovered these things by a system of trial and error. As you practise your social skills in youth, you come to recognise which approaches to other people have the best results and you retain them. Equally, you reject things which bring bad results.

For instance, if you should meet someone at a party who pins you in a corner and talks incessantly the whole evening on a subject that doesn't interest you, you can say with some certainty that your tormentor has an underdeveloped social skill: i.e. he cannot make good conversation. If he is sensitive, he will go home and think about why you were yawning and looking over his shoulder and making excuses to be elsewhere in the room when he was trying so hard to make friends with you. He might well come to the conclusion that he didn't let you get a word in edgeways, that he didn't check that you were interested in what he was saying, and that his body language was making you uncomfortable. To most people this will seem obvious, but to those who lack social skills it will not be so clear. Next time you meet this man at a party, he will hopefully have given some thought to what went wrong and resolve that he won't pin you in a corner, and that he will make an effort to find out something about *you* as well as talking about his own interests.

Research into small-talk (despised by many, but an essential preliminary to more meaningful friendships) indicate that it is most effective (measured by the impression left on the participants) if it is approximately a fifty-fifty split. So, if you want to make a good impression on someone you've just met informally, then let them talk for half the time and you talk the rest. (Which is not to say that if the conversation lasts for half an hour, you talk for the first fifteen minutes and he talks for the other fifteen. Ping-Pong is the answer, pass the initiative back and forth between you.)

The next point to remember is that generally people do not like you to reveal too much about yourself too soon, and you shouldn't expect *them* to lay their heart on the line at the first encounter either. Most of us have met people who have wanted to "spill their guts" on the initial meeting. They tell us about their failed love affair or about their sexual difficulties and, while it may be fascinating, the likelihood is that we will not choose that person as a friend. We need to explore each other's opinions and feelings gradually, so at the first meeting reveal just a little bit about yourself, and allow your conversation partner to reveal only as much as he or she is comfortable with. Tell each other more or less the same amount of personal information. It's OK to talk about non-sensitive subjects, like what kind of work you do, what type of food you prefer or where you like to go for evenings out. Once you've started feeling comfortable talking to each other, you can proceed into other areas which are a little more intimate. But take it slowly, and don't probe too deeply at first. Your conversation partner will let you know - either directly or in some other subtle way - if there is an area that he or she doesn't want to talk about. Look for signs of discomfort and change the topic.

But the shy person might say: "How on earth do you start in the first place? I just get tongue-tied."

If you're at a gay party or in a gay bar, then it's pretty safe to talk about gay things: a programme you saw on television about coming out, or the new play about Aids. You could discuss a book you've read recently on a gay theme or talk about the latest clubs and what kind of music they play. By gentle probing you can discover what your prospective friend likes. If you like the same things, great. But if he or she indicates that they're interested in something you know nothing about, here's your opportunity to learn. If it's a topic that bores you rigid, then perhaps it would be better to make your excuses and try elsewhere, but, if you genuinely want to know more, ask them questions about whatever it is that turns them on.

So, your friend is into hang-gliding, but you don't even know what it is. Ask for an explanation. Then follow this up with other questions which show that you are interested in finding our more (if you are). Where does he do this hang-gliding? Is he a member of a club? Is it an expensive hobby? Is it dangerous? Can anybody do it or does it need special training?

Of course, you'll ask these questions in a naturally progressing way. People who use this technique of hitting a person's "hot button" (as asking them about things that interest them is called) sometimes mistakenly give them the third degree. One question follows another in rapid succession with no information passing the other way.

Here is Mike, who's been invited to John's party. Mike is pretty anxious about the party, because he knows John mixes with an interesting group of people and he's worried that he'll not match up to their vivacity. He feels he can't make small-talk, doesn't know how to sustain conversations after the initial introduction, and is convinced that he has absolutely nothing of interest to say. Over in the corner he sees Ralph, standing alone with his drink. Ralph looks friendly and is fairly attractive, so Mike takes his courage in both hands and walks across the room:

"Hi, my name's Mike"
"Hello, I'm Ralph."
"It's a nice party, isn't it?"
"Yes. A good selection of people."
" How did you come to know John?"
"Oh, we met at the hang-gliding club."
"Hang-gliding? What's that?"

"It's a newish sport. You strap yourself into this contraption with wings and rudders and launch yourself from a high place."

"Really? Is it dangerous?"

"It can be if you don't know what you're doing."

" Have you been doing it long?"

"A couple of years."

"Is it expensive to hang-glide?"

"It can be if you get all the right equipment."

"Have you ever been hurt?"

"Only once. I lost control on take-off."

"What did you do?"

"Broke a leg."

"Did it take long to recover?"

"I was in hospital about two weeks"

"Which hospital?"

"Oh, the local General Hospital."

"Which ward were you in?"...

This kind of intense questioning becomes, after a while, irritating and even threatening. It isn't conversation at all, it's an inquisition. If it is accompanied by an unremitting stare, standing too close with no escape route for the victim, then it becomes actively unpleasant and unendurable.

By all means express an interest in what interests other people, but give them chance to get their breath occasionally by letting them know something about yourself (even if it's only your opinion about what they're saying).

If you find you're getting on to controversial topics, or subjects you don't agree about, you have to make the decision either to terminate the conversation ("Excuse me, I must go and get another drink/ find the lavatory/ start making tracks"); change the subject ("What do you think of this chandelier?");

or state quite calmly that you don't approve of what is being said ("I don't like this kind of racist talk").

So, let's run that conversation again:

"Hi, my name's Mike."

"Hello, Mike, I'm Ralph."

"It's a great party, isn't it?"

"And a lovely mix of people."

"Are you a friend of John's?"

"Yes, we met at a hang-gliding club."

"Really? I didn't know he was into that. I met him at the local pub. To be honest, I don't really know what hang-gliding is."

"Oh, it's hanging on to a one-man glider contraption. It's made of steel tubes and plastic sheeting. You launch yourself from a high place, and there you are, gliding."

"Goodness, that sounds exciting. I'll bet it's ever so exhilarating."

"Yes, you get sort of addicted to it. It's great for giving you a high."

"I remember going in a glider plane once, and that was pretty exciting. But I was just a passenger. I expect it's quite different to being in complete control and exposed to the elements."

"You say you met John at a pub, which one was that?"

"The Red Lion. Do you know it?"

"That's the gay pub on the High Street?"

"Yes. I don't care for it much myself, but there aren't many places to go around here. The music gets a bit loud and it's difficult to talk."

"Why do they do that? How on earth are you supposed to have a conversation when you can hardly hear yourself think?"

"I wouldn't mind so much, but their choice of music leaves a lot to be desired. If they'd just mix it a bit instead of playing heavy rock the whole time."

"Do you like to dance?"

"Yes."

"Come on then, let's show them how it's done."

The conversation in the second attempt flowed much more naturally and freely. Both participants got to know something about the other, but neither were made uncomfortable by the conversation being one-sided or intrusive.

On The Gay Scene

If you're making your first foray into a gay bar, you will probably be nervous and excited at the same time. In the bars the etiquette is somewhat different to that at parties or in smaller groups. Often the atmosphere in gay pubs and clubs is "cruisy" - everyone is on the look-out for potential partners and the approach can be more direct. For the shy and unskilled, this can be an extremely frightening prospect: what if he should be rebuffed or rejected? For those with low self-esteem, this is really the worst possible thing they could imagine. Indeed, a survey recently asked "What is the thing you fear most in personal relationships?" and the top answer was "rejection".

Those who have plenty of confidence and a high self-esteem will survive unscathed when they make an approach and the answer is "no thanks". For others who aren't so secure, a rejection can be a devastating experience that leaves them feeling that their whole being has been flattened.

When we take risks we need to prepare ourselves for possible negative consequences. If you have decided that you are going to strike up a conversation with someone and you don't know how they'll respond, then mentally prepare yourself for all eventualities before you step in. If he turns out to be friendly and receptive, then ensure that you know how you're going to develop the approach (perhaps by offering to buy him a drink or to compliment him on something that you like the look of - his style in clothes or hair cut, for instance). If he should smile wanly and tell you, either kindly or brutally, that he isn't interested, then be prepared for that too. Before you go in, give yourself a little pep-talk, on these lines: "If he says no, then that's OK, it's his prerogative. It doesn't mean that I'm a total nonentity who nobody could ever find attractive, it simply means that he has his reasons for not wanting to respond tonight. I might feel the same about someone else on another occasion. Don't get upset, just shrug your shoulders and try again somewhere else."

Preparing yourself beforehand for the possibility of rejection can make it much easier to bear if it comes. If the rejection is insensitive and insulting, don't take it to heart - such an ill-mannered response to your overtures of friendship reflect much more badly on the person who uttered them than on you.

The music in pubs and bars can be extremely loud (and seems to be becoming louder and louder each week), and it can be difficult in those places to make any kind of conversation. Much of your initial contact will have to be by facial expression and body language. Once you get close to the object of your desires, it will be possible to shout in his ear to be heard over the music, and occasionally there are quiet corners in pubs where you can really talk to each other. Sometimes this won't be necessary - occasionally just the exchange of glances, smiles and a nod of the head can be enough to set the relationship in motion. He likes the look of you, you like the look of him. The next question is: your place or his.

Remember, too, that body language plays an important role in these situations. Try to appear open and receptive. There'll be more information on this later in the chapter.

We often pick people up in pubs and clubs simply because we like the look of them. There is little opportunity to get to know them before the decision has to be made whether or not to invite them home. It's when we have to see them in the cold light of day, away from the drinks and lights and throbbing music that disillusionment might set in. Sometimes it all works out fine, but occasionally the good looks that were so appealing in the club hide an unpleasant or boring personality. The "morning after" scenario is familiar to most gay men and it goes like this: "crumbs, what a mistake I made inviting *him* to stay the night. How can I get him out of the flat at the earliest possible moment without hurting his feelings?"

Not a very respectful way to treat each other, but if the feelings are honest, it should be possible to admit the mistake and sever the relationship without being too nasty and hurtful about it. The rules of assertiveness apply in this situation, as in any other. If he wants to see you again but you don't really want to see him, it is far better to be honest and state your feelings sensitively than to make vague promises that you have no intention of keeping.

Why say: "Yes, I'll call you and we'll arrange something" when what you mean is: "Sorry, I don't think this is going to work. But it was very nice meeting you."

If he is persistent, you can always use the broken record technique. Remember, though, you aren't obliged to explain your feelings if you don't want to. All the same, a truly assertive person would be particularly caring in this sensitive area of human relationships. As we've seen, people can be easily hurt and their self-esteem easily damaged by brutal rejections. You don't, I'm sure, appreciate people treating you cruelly, so try hard not to inflict hurt on others.

The gay scene has long had a reputation for sometimes being ruthless and unpleasant. It is up to all of us to treat each other more gently and respectfully.

The Non-Commercial Option

An alternative to the pub and club scene are the gay social groups run by volunteers on a non-commercial basis. The sole reason for the existence of these groups is to help people find friends in an environment that is less pushy, noisy and sexually charged than the commercial scene. There are groups in most parts of the country, although in the big cities there are more of them to choose from. Find out what's available in your area by looking in the listings pages of magazines like *Gay Times*. Often these groups will make a big effort to welcome people new to the gay scene. Once you've gained a few friends in this way, and your confidence begins to build, the commercial scene might not seem such a daunting prospect.

Talking to people at parties and groups, or in pubs and clubs is one thing, but if you want to develop the friendship, you will have to share more than just conversation. Why not ask someone you have made a breakthrough with to go to the cinema with you, or come round to your place for a meal? Not necessarily for sex, but just so you can talk about things and get to know each other better?

Once again, those who are less than confident might find this a challenge. Because they are afraid of rejection they hesitate to ask people out. "Why on earth would he want to go out with me?" the person with low self-esteem might say. "What have I got to offer in the way of friendship?"

And again, the fear of rejection looms large. "If I ask him if he'd like to go to the theatre with me, he might say no and I'd feel like an idiot for even suggesting it."

Once again, prepare yourself for all eventualities before asking your new contact if he'd like to go out with you. Take courage from the knowledge that everyone is looking for friends. Very few of us feel that we have enough friends within our circle, and if someone shows an interest, we may well feel flattered and happy. It's worth taking the risk - if you don't, you'll never know whether you've missed out on a lovely friendship.

Making A Start

Friendships need nurturing, too, if they are to survive. Keeping in touch is important. Let's look at this scenario: Ben has met Frank at a wine and cheese party organised by his local gay group. They talked easily at the party, and shared a lot of interests. During their conversation, Ben had indicated that he was interested in seeing a new film that had just come out. Frank said he'd like to see it, too. So Ben gave Frank his phone number and said: "Call me and we'll arrange something."

But then Ben had gone off to talk to other people, and Frank wasn't sure that he really meant it. Now he had this telephone number, but was wary of dialling it. Suppose Ben was just being polite and didn't really wanted to see the film with him? Maybe the phone call would embarrass or annoy him. Frank didn't know how he would react if Ben suddenly decided that he didn't want to do it after all, and had jut been fobbing him off with the phone number in order to get rid of him. All the old insecurities about rejection had come up again.

In the end, Frank decided that he would have to take the chance. Ben had been really nice to him at the party, and seemed genuinely friendly, so it was unlikely that he would suddenly turn into a rude and rejecting monster.

"I dialled Ben's number, and he seemed really pleased to hear from me. I mentioned that he'd expressed an interest in this film and he said: 'Yes, when do you want to go?' I was thrilled, and we made an arrangement to meet. I knew that Ben wasn't interested in me sexually, but we went on from there to be really good friends. He said that he often went to the cinema on his own because he couldn't find anyone who shared his interest in these rather esoteric films. We had a great time, and went out for a meal afterwards. Actually I had eaten before I set out, but I was enjoying myself so much that I went and ate another meal just so that we could spend some more time together. The conversation was effortless. Ben is very easy to talk to. I've begun to secretly analyse how he does it, so that I can pick up a few tips. There never seems to be any awkward silences in Ben's conversation like there are in mine, and he always seems genuinely interested in whatever's under discussion. I felt great afterwards. I'd made my first gay friend, and I was determined that we would develop this friendship. So later I rang him again and suggested that we go out dancing to a gay club one night. He was very responsive and said he'd call me the next day. And so he did, and we've been talking on the phone just about every day since then."

After two years Frank and Ben's friendship is still going strong. They've both had lovers since they met, but they've kept contact with each other and shared their experiences. They've grown together through this time, and each feels much more secure knowing that he can depend on the other.

Frank and Ben live only a mile away from each other, and keeping in touch is not difficult. They often call on each other, pop in for cups of tea or spend the evening watching a video which interests them both. Their shared experiences are now beginning to grow in number and their friendship is starting to accumulate a history.

They are both of the opinion that if they didn't live so close to each other it would be difficult for them to keep the friendship going. Both have had friendships with other people which have faltered because they lived too far away to have much physical contact. Research seems to support the idea that friendships conducted at a distance don't often work as well as those with people who are easily accessible to us.

Body Language

Once again, body language can help you in making your breakthrough into friendship. A smile, on making that first approach, reassures people that you're friendly. An open body posture tells them that you are approachable. Don't sit with legs crossed and arms folded - this indicates that you want to be left alone. Uncross your legs, keep your arms down and your hands away from your face. Sit up straight, look alert and relaxed and people will know instantly that it's safe to say hello.

If, after having talked to them for a while, you want to let someone know that you are interested in them, you can mirror their movements. If they take a drink, you take a drink; if they cross their legs, you cross your legs; if they laugh, you laugh and so on. If you do this subtly, your partner will unconsciously take in from you the signal that you find them attractive. If, however, you simply copy everything they do in exactly the same way, immediately after they do it, they'll think you're mad.

You can also assess *their* interest in *you* by noticing whether they are mirroring any of your gestures.

Personal space is important. In most Western cultures, a space of about eighteen inches is what most people feel comfortable with. If you stand closer than this when you're conversing with someone, they'll either step back to increase the space or, if they can't do that, they'll feel extremely uncomfortable. Another test of whether someone is finding you sexually interesting is to invade their personal space - gradually move closer to them than the eighteen inches - and see their reaction. If they don't try to increase the space between you, then they're interested, but if they step back, it's likely that you're barking up the wrong tree.

Remember the other rules which we've already looked at: don't stare intently into people's eyes for long periods - this is threatening (unless you are in love with them and they with you, in which case it will be a highly pleasurable experience). Use hand gestures to animate your conversation, by all means, but don't forget that jabbing or wagging fingers signal disapproval.

Human interaction is highly complex, and those who communicate inappropriately with their fellow men are likely to feel very isolated. If you feel you would benefit from improving your skills in this area, then it is worthwhile to take time to analyse what particular aspect you need to concentrate on. Buy a few books on communication skills, body language and overcoming shyness.

Assertiveness can help you if you're shy. Think back over the rules of assertiveness and remember that you can use some of these techniques in your friendly interactions, too. If you always feel inferior in conversations then try a few of the assertiveness techniques which will help you come across as more relaxed and less retiring.

Most of all it needs practise. There will be failures, and for those who are crushed by rejection this can be the hardest part. Try to learn from your mistakes rather than being defeated by them. If one approach fails, then don't internalise it, analyse it. Then try another. In his leaflet *Counselling Homosexuals* (Bedford Square Press), Peter Righton wrote: "the only way people learn to relate to one another is by meeting and continuing to meet. Only when an isolated homosexual exposes his vulnerability to another person in a genuine encounter and gains, through constantly repeated meetings, a growing sense of being accepted for the person he is, can he begin to learn that life holds more for him than rejection, indifference or hostility."

Eventually, almost imperceptibly, you will begin to make progress, and if you stick at it, you'll gradually accumulate a circle of friends who will support you when the going gets rough.

8: RELATIONSHIPS

Something like 95 per cent of the population marry at some point in their life. This indicates that either (a) long-term, committed relationships satisfy a profound need in human beings or that (b) social conditioning is so powerful that it is, for the most part, irresistible.

Most gay people grow up in the warm glow (or dark shadow) of their parents' marriage. If they were lucky enough to come from a happy family, it is likely that they will have positive ideas of what a long-term relationship can offer; they may have a strong desire to have a relationship like that of their parents. Others, who have been subjected to a miserable home life, where parents disliked or even hated each other, might want to leave such arrangements far behind.

Although there is not the same pressure on gay people as there is on heterosexuals to "settle down", the choices that such freedom brings us can be bewildering. It isn't always easy to know what we want from our gay life - perhaps a one-to-one relationship, perhaps a degree of emotional autonomy or maybe some combination of both. Mistakes are easily made when subtle pressures are at work in our subconscious. Past experiences can give us a false idea of what is the best or worst way for us to live.

Are we, for instance, entering into a relationship because we think we "should"? Or are we avoiding relationships, even though we want them, because we are afraid of the commitment and the possible consequences on our lives? It is, after all, much harder to stay in the closet when there are two of you living together. People tend to put two and two together and get "gay".

And so, although we have more choices about the kinds of lifestyles we can lead, we also have more factors to take into account in making our decision. If we are to make an informed and honest choice, we need a reasonably high level of gay self-esteem. And, of course, circumstances change, needs alter and feelings don't always remain constant. Spending time mastering the art of being comfortable on our own and being self-sufficient in all major areas of life will ensure that if we do decide to enter into a relationship, it will be because we want to and not simply through fear of being alone.

Ted is a gay man who has a fantasy of having a partner to live with and love. He has always thought that one day it would be lovely just to have a quiet little home somewhere, where his lover would be waiting to welcome him and comfort him and provide relief from the loneliness that he has felt for most of his life. But whenever the chance of such a relationship comes along, Ted sabotages it. He always has a convincing "reason" why he can't make a commitment. Here are some of the excuses Ted has given to lovers who were getting too close to fitting his fantasy:

"I'm sorry, Rory, but I've just got so used to living on my own I couldn't possibly share my space with someone else - I've become too selfish."

"I'm terribly sorry, Tony, you know I love you and I wish we could make something of it, but I'm just not ready to settle down yet."

"David, sweetheart, you're the best thing that ever happened to me, but it would never work. We're far too intense, and I'd like to step back."

Ted knows he could have made a go of a relationship with any of these men if only he'd had the courage to do it. But when it came to the crunch he backed off because he wasn't ready to face the consequences of such a commitment. He knew that if he moved into their home or they moved into his, questions would be asked almost immediately. What is the nature of the relationship between two unmarried men in their thirties living together? It would be difficult for him to keep his sexuality under wraps as he had successfully done so far. Although the closet is a lonely place, he reasoned, at least it offers protection from persecution and confrontations.

Ted is not making an honest choice about his lifestyle. He is avoiding what he wants most of all because he is afraid of change and possible pain.

The same thing is happening in reverse to Danny. He is involved in a relationship with Frank. They muddle along amiably, but Danny is tormented by the thought that his life is stunted, and he longs for adventure.

Danny met Frank almost as soon as he came on to the gay scene. They were immediately attracted and became lovers. Danny had felt that once he was in a settled relationship, things would be easier. There would be someone to support him and, when he had come out to his parents, his mother had said: "I don't want you to be lonely. I hope you'll meet someone you can make a go of it with." He had proudly taken Frank home to meet his parents. They all got on well together, and Danny was happy that his mother liked Frank. He felt that he had put her mind at rest on this particular topic - he wasn't going to be a lonely old man!

And yet, two years on, Danny feels trapped. He would love to have a place of his own, where he can make his own decisions without reference to anyone else. He doesn't blame Frank for these feelings, he's still very fond of him. But Danny wants out of the relationship. Not just this relationship, but any relationship. He doesn't want to be one half of a couple, he wants to have friends and lovers, and to explore as he likes. He finds the relationship with Frank confining, and he hates having to discuss his every move. But he stays. His excuses?

"At least the relationship prevents me from being lonely. I don't know whether I would be able to survive living on my own."

"I'm doing what everyone says I should - settling down and being respectable."

"It would be selfish of me to hurt Frank by breaking up the relationship when he is obviously so happy."

Danny hasn't realised yet that gay people have infinitely more choices than most straight people do. He can still have his relationship with Frank, but they don't have to live together. He can explore the single state if that's what he wants to do, and if he has a support network of gay friends, he won't feel he's the odd one out because he isn't half of a couple. Unattached people aren't out on a limb at the average gay dinner party, as they would be at most straight ones.

Like Ted, Danny is not making an honest choice. He is influenced by "shoulds" ('people should find a partner and settle down'). Assertive people don't accept "should" messages from others.

Although it isn't always easy to know whether a relationship is right for you, don't forget that mistakes can be corrected. If you enter into a relationship that doesn't work out, then try to learn something from the experience. Be honest about what makes you happy and what makes you uncomfortable. If life with a loving, long-time partner gives you a warm, rosy glow, then don't let other people persuade you that it isn't "politically correct" or "safe" to pursue that relationship. Equally, if the idea of a cosy little home for two makes you want to run a mile, don't feel pressured into a domestic set-up that isn't for you.

We have to make the rules up as we go along, which is a liberation for some people and a dilemma for others.

Power Sharing

Most people want the power in their relationship to be shared equally; for them, any significant imbalance which cannot be corrected will lead to frustration, resentment and maybe the eventual breakdown of the relationship. Friction and unpleasantness will inevitably ensue when one of the partners constantly feels that he has to subordinate his needs to the other. It isn't always easy for those involved in the relationship to analyse when there is an imbalance of power, and so rows and arguments often lead nowhere because the real problem isn't recognised or simply isn't confronted. Attaining and maintaining that balance in the face of constantly shifting circumstances is quite a skill, and most people do it unconsciously. Some, though, haven't mastered the art and need to make special efforts.

The power structure in most healthy relationships is fluid, passing from one partner to another, depending on circumstances. Most partners recognise the necessity of this and will tolerate the temporary reduction in their power because they know it will be of overall benefit to the relationship. For instance, one partner might be better at negotiating financial deals, and so the other will be willing to step back and allow his loved one to take over the arrangement of a mortgage or loan. They may have agreed beforehand what they want, but the actual deal-making will be left to the partner who is better able to handle it. When the deal is finalised, power-sharing returns to its previous egalitarian state, and any other situation which might require one partner to step out of the limelight for a while can be negotiated.

In Love With Your Best Friend

The good news is that gay relationships have a great capacity for equality. Unlike their heterosexual equivalent, gay relationships are mainly based on the "best friend" principle, rather than the hierarchical "man and wife" model of heterosexuals. Many straight people like to think that gay relationships work on the basis of being a pretend marriage, with one man playing the role of the husband and the other the subordinate role of the "wife". It makes the whole thing easier for them to understand. In reality, however, such a set-up is extremely rare in Western cultures.

There is no pre-ordained power-structure in gay partnerships, as there tends to be in heterosexual marriage, and any power-structure which emerges will have been created by the participants - not by society. It follows that we will be able to change that power-structure if it becomes unevenly shared.

Gay people have to be tough to overcome the hurdles which stand in the way of their relationships - just finding each other in the first place is no mean achievement, especially when you consider the lengths that society goes to discourage us from even exploring our sexuality. Setting up in a gay relationship involves defying convention, and that isn't easy at any time.

Given that our relationships are under such pressure, it isn't really surprising that so many of them fail to survive for as long as was originally hoped for. The advantage that we do have - being able to achieve a power-balance that most male-female relationships lack - can be undermined when the partners don't have similarly developed senses of self-esteem.

I have written at length about gay relationships in my book *Making Gay Relationships Work* and if you are in a relationship which is in need of repair or improvement, then I suggest you and your partner read it. The book covers such topics as negotiation, communication, sexual difficulties and recognising when a relationship is changing.

Changing The Rules Can Be Problematic

Applying assertiveness to intimate relationships is, perhaps, the most difficult area of all. Any changes made in the power balance between you and your partner need to be made sensitively so that you do not create any feelings of resentment or manipulation. If a partnership has existed over a long period with a particular balance and ethos, then any attempt to change it could cause great insecurity for both partners. As we've already discovered, none of us like change, but occasionally it is inevitable and necessary for the health of everyone concerned. If you can rid your relationship of any persistent feelings which lead to rows, sulks, resentment and a sense of helplessness, then both of you will ultimately benefit. But remember - your partner, who is going to be on the receiving end of your new assertive behaviours, may react with fear, bewilderment or aggression. If he has become used to having his own way, dictating the terms and making unilateral decisions about your mutual interests, he might resist this new, assertive you.

Perhaps it is fairer if you discuss with your partner your intention to behave differently. Explain your purpose and ensure that he knows that it is not meant as a threat to him and that hopefully it will result in an improvement in the quality of your relationship. Ask him to help you by being receptive. Make sure he understands that assertiveness is not about "turning the tables", but about equality. From now on you are going to analyse where you stand in the relationship, and try to pinpoint those aspects of your life together that bring on feelings of dissatisfaction or even depression. You are going to ensure that your true needs are expressed and taken into account when making decisions which affect you both.

He may not be happy about being told that his behaviour has been less than exemplary, but you can explain to him in an assertive way where you think the problem lies. You can also deal assertively with any reactions of outrage or hurt. He might say: "You make me out to be a tyrant! I haven't locked you in your room or taken away your free will. How come suddenly it's all my fault? You're no angel yourself." Try to reassure him that you are not presenting yourself as being completely free of blame - after all, you went along with the arrangements up until now. Simply explain that from now on you'd like things to be a little different. Tell him that you don't want to take anything away from him, and that your intentions are constructive. He may play the injured or insulted party in an attempt to make you drop your plans. That, of course, would be your first challenge. You are making a pact with yourself to resist any further attempts to be treated as an emotional inferior. You have rights, too! Refer back to the Golden Rules in Chapter Three.

After a long time - maybe years - of behaving in one way, you might have difficulty changing to another. After denying your needs for so long, or putting your decisions into the hands of someone else, you may have problems isolating exactly what it is that you want from your relationship - or even what your opinion is on any given topic. These are the skills you need to work on. For instance, if your partner always makes the holiday arrangements for you both (after having agreed vaguely what it is that you both want to do that year), then perhaps it's time you were more specific about your own wants.

The conversation might go like this:

"What shall we do for our holiday this year?"

"I haven't thought about it."

"Have you got any preferences?"

"I don't mind really."

"Do you fancy doing a different area of France this time?"

"I suppose we could."

"Any suggestions about which area?"

"It doesn't really make much difference to me."

"Shall we take the car and tour or would you prefer a package holiday?"

"They both sound OK."

Based on this information, your lover goes out and books the holiday *he* wants, on the assumption that you'll be happy with it.

When he presents it as a *fait accompli* you say in a sarcastic voice: "Oh, we're going on the ferry again, are we?" and then begin to sulk.

"Is something wrong?" he asks.

"Oh no. Nothing at all. Although you're perfectly well aware that I hate boats, and they always make me ill. Still, I suppose I'll have to put up with it."

An assertive response to his initial question about holidays might have been: "I'd much rather we flew to France this year instead of going on the ferry. I dread that journey, it always makes me seasick and spoils the start of the trip." Or, if the reason you're being obtuse about the whole thing is because you don't really want to go to France at all - or even on holiday - then it is far better if you can say so up front.

There may have to be discussion, but at least you've put your cards on the table.

Changing Behaviour Upsets People

Attempting to equalise the balance of power in a long-established relationship will inevitably lead to conflict, but that should not be a reason to avoid the attempt. Welcome creative conflict as an opportunity to air problems and, hopefully, resolve them. Rows that may be sparked by your sudden change of attitude will give you the opportunity to discuss what you're trying to do, and to ensure that the other person realises that you are determined to make changes.

The last thing we want is for your relationship to be turned into a battleground - that's not what a loving partnership is about. So, try to negotiate as much as possible without aggression. Don't respond in kind to aggressive reactions. Re-read the elements of assertiveness from earlier chapters and put them into effect.

As we have said assertiveness, remember, is a method of allowing you to state your opinions and needs without feeling badly about it. Be sensitive to your partner's fears and confusion over this new version of you, and give him as much reassurance as he needs.

Bear in mind that you don't have to be assertive all the time. You can choose your moments and your issues. It may be that only those aspects of your relationship which make you feel uncomfortable need to be re-thought from an assertive perspective. After all, it can sometimes be pleasant to sit back and let someone else take charge. So, if your boyfriend is a particularly good cook, you may be happy to let him rule the roost in the kitchen, or if he is a lousy cook, you may now be able to tell him in the most effective way that you'd like to take over - without having to be hurtful about it.

A relationship is a two-way arrangement and it should never be forgotten that assertiveness is about allowing the other person their dignity and opinions, too. The constantly shifting power-base in most relationships is mostly self-correcting, it is only when there are distinct feelings of resentment or manipulation that changes need to be made— and one of those changes could be assertiveness.

As Claire Walmsley wrote in her book on assertiveness: "In relationships that are special, we owe it to each other to be honest. Caring about people and loving them, means we should feel free to behave in an honest and open manner."

Communication Is The Key

Any agony aunt or counsellor will tell you that communication is the key to good relationships. Communication is also the key to effective assertiveness. We've already said that direct, clear and unambiguous statements are most likely to get you the results you are seeking, without hostile reactions. This goes for relationships, too. When trying to state your needs or feelings, don't try to cover up by going round the houses to say what you have to say. Speak directly, honestly and as clearly as you can. This is not, of course, *carte blanche* for brutality or insensitivity. Your lover's feelings are as important as yours, and deserve to be respected. If an unpleasant truth needs to be spoken, then it shouldn't be avoided, but neither should it be phrased in such a way that it wounds.

Arguments are a legitimate way of bringing nagging problems to the surface and airing them (and hopefully resolving them), but arguments should aim to be creative.

Neither partner in an argument should use it as an opportunity to lacerate the other with irrelevant and hurtful comments about other issues. Sometimes, though, arguments get heated and complaints are aired in less than sensitive ways. This is better than not airing them at all. If your relationship is strong in other ways it is likely that it will survive the occasional hastily spoken insult or barb, so long as the intention was good. It is far better to occasionally let rip at your partner than to be too "nice" and over-sensitive. If you can clear the air constructively, and then make up, you're well on the way to having the love of your life.

The ability to communicate honestly and truthfully with each other is a sign of a successful partnership. Here are fifteen more points to help you understand what genuine communication is about and how to use it more effectively with your partner:

1. It needs to be accepted that true communication is risky. You may have spent a long time talking to each other in rather ritualistic ways which avoid the core of problems. By skirting round the real issues, confrontation is avoided and some kind of status quo is sustained. That, however, does not achieve our objective - which is to remove the resentment that can stand in the way of our loving each other unequivocally. If you talk *round* the issue instead of *to* it, then nothing changes. If someone gets too near the problem, the other might avoid it by sulking or walking away or playing other manipulative games. Don't avoid confronting problems, however painful they may be. Avoidance only prolongs the agony.

2. You must both *care* if communication is to happen. You must care about each other and about your relationship. If either of you is indifferent, then there is unlikely to be any real communication and little prospect of getting to the source of troubles. Indifference indicates a fundamental problem with the relationship, which may be terminal.

3. Each of you must be willing to work on problems that are worrying you, and to do so honestly. It's no good if only one of you is prepared to be honest and open. You must both be prepared to disclose your feelings about the issue under discussion, and to trust the other with your feelings. If you aren't, then there won't be progress. You must both be prepared to give plenty of time to the matter.

4. Make sure you have enough time and privacy to discuss your problems. Don't start an important negotiation or discussion just before you have to set out for work, or at some other time when you know you will be interrupted.

5. Both must listen carefully to what the other is saying. A good way to check this is to *feed back* what the other has said as accurately as you can. Don't try to change the meaning of what was said - your partner must be satisfied that what you have fed back to him is an accurate account of what he said. This is the very core of communication skills, to really understand and accept what the other person has said about the way he feels.

6. It is important that when partners are communicating they become "the same psychological size", accepting each other's ideas and feelings with respect. Any attempt to pull rank, claim intellectual superiority, manipulate with guilt or to play any other kind of 'game' will immediately undermine the communication and make it less effective.

7. Much more attention and energy needs to be focused on feelings and values. Own your feelings. Try to say "I feel..." rather than "You feel..." Accept what other people say about their feelings without being judgmental or critical. Don't say things like: "You can't possibly think that..." or "That's not the way you feel".

It's very easy to talk in a formalised way, using words as a shield to deflect attention away from what we truly feel. That turns out to be just "talk"; what we want is "communication" - a very different proposition. Don't be ashamed of what you feel, even if it isn't what the other person wants to hear. Don't try to make your feelings into someone else's responsibility. Don't say: "You make me feel bad", say "I feel bad because..."

8. An honest sharing of feelings - which is what communication amounts to - does not give permission to be brutal. Honesty does not mean getting revenge or hurting people. Being 'brutally honest' about other people's deepest feelings is an aggressive not an assertive way of communicating. Painful truths can be told gently and be accompanied with reassurance. If you are angry, say so: don't say: "You make me feel angry..." but "I feel angry because..."

Communication won't always provide a solution, but neither should it result in a "winner". If communication and negotiation is to be effective, then it has to be a "win-win" outcome.

9. Communication means that we are trying to *empathise* - which means attempting to get inside the other person's skin and trying to truly understand what he or she is feeling. It's much more than sympathising - it is an attempt to actually *feel* what the other is feeling, even if only for a moment or two. This will give greater insight into what is happening between you. Be generous in your interpretation of behaviour. You are not there to approve, disapprove, to label or explain anyone's feelings, any more than they should do yours. Remember that people can grow and change, and honest communication can help them to do that.

10. Communication is not just about talking to each other or trying to interpret each other's body language - it goes much deeper than that. It is logical and illogical, verbal and non-verbal. It is as complex as human experience. Don't try to invent a set of rules for how people "should" feel. Our emotions do not always follow a fixed and predictable pattern. Be prepared for people to be contradictory and try to accept it. The great gay poet Walt Whitman wrote: "Do I contradict myself? / Very well then I contradict myself / (I am large, I contain multitudes)."

11. With patience and commitment, communication is possible between people who appear at first sight to have little in common. With goodwill, it is possible to communicate over the generation gap, over ethnic differences, and between straight people and gay people. Prejudices can be overcome through communication.

12. Communication is not a quick and easy skill to master. If you have been used to intellectualising your actions and motives, then you might find changing to a more feelings-based method of communication difficult. Persevere, it's worth it in the end.

13. Words are not always precise. If, when you are communicating with someone, you feel you may have misunderstood or are not clear, then say so. Saying "Did you mean...?" or "Could you explain that a little more, I'm confused..." is better than floundering in the dark or trying to guess and getting it wrong.

14. Formal education and a person's ability to put labels on their actions and motives often act as a barrier to communication. If everything we say or do and everything we feel needs to be explained and have a name, then we will not be able to communicate very effectively. For instance, if a film leaves you unmoved but has your partner in floods of tears, you might say "That's just sentimental nonsense". In using that label you have *intellectualised* the feelings and devalued them. It is impossible to communicate about them, because they have now been given a label which might not be accurate. The film may have provided a trigger, but who knows where the feelings came from? Will they be any the less sincere just because we think we can explain them? Those tears have probably got a long history, but it is counterproductive to explain them instead of just accepting their sincerity.

15. There are many benefits from improved communication, two important ones are:
Verification: being clear that you both understand what is going on between you. If you have spent the night worrying because your partner is silent and withdrawn, an honest communication can help reassure you by verifying what the problem is, and whether it is connected with you.
Clarity of meaning: misunderstandings in relationships can cause tremendous anxiety. If we have ensured that we truly understand what our partner is saying - by clarifying it with him, then that unnecessary anxiety is dissipated.

Genuine and well-intentioned communication will help rid your relationship of the destructive elements of doubt, anger and anxiety. It is clear from the descriptions we've given that real communication does not involve manipulation, guilt-inducement, indirectness or misleading behaviour.

While you are aiming to make your relationship more satisfying, equal and fulfilling by communicating well, there is no need to be overly "nice". Indeed, too much niceness can be a form of aggression or a means of avoiding the legitimate exploration of problems. "I can't tell him that I'm not happy with our sex life, it would hurt him so much," thinks the overly-sensitive lover who is anxious not to hurt the object of his affection. And so the problem remains unconfronted.

Applying assertiveness to personal relationships can bring to them a new sense of fairness and equality. When both partners feel free to say what they want, safe to express doubts and dissatisfactions without fear of reprisal, then the relationship is functioning well. Those who are assertive in their intimate relationships are well aware that the only way for both partners to be happy is for an honest exchange of feelings and an equally honest acceptance of the validity of each other's needs.

Here are a few techniques that non-assertive lovers might use to control each other or get their own way. Think carefully about these behaviours, and if you recognise any of them in your own relationship, then try hard to eliminate them.

1. Passive Aggression

When a non-assertive person doesn't want to do something that's been asked, but doesn't know how to say "no", he might use the techniques which seem passive, but which are, in fact, really aggressive, to get his way.

"Forgetting" or "misunderstanding" are two classic forms of passive aggression. For instance, suppose you have discussed redecorating your home with your partner and in response have received the non-committal "I don't mind" or "It doesn't really matter to me" response. You go ahead with arrangements which you imagine you had agreed between you and ask: "As you're passing the D-I-Y shop on the way home from work, would you mind getting the off-white paint so that I can start re-painting the dining room?"

Your partner conveniently "forgets" to get the paint or comes back with something totally different to the one you mentioned. Instead of saying directly: "I don't really want to do any decorating" or "I don't like this colour scheme", he tells you in an indirect way by these obstructions.

Another passive-aggressive technique is procrastination. There may be an issue which is important to one partner, but which is of little interest to the other. Instead of expressing this lack of interest directly, the passive-aggressive partner will procrastinate and put it off, making excuses to buy time, hoping that by moving at a snail's pace the issue will go away.

Persistent late-coming is another form of passive aggression. It is a way to indirectly exert power over someone by arranging to meet them and then arriving late. Keeping people waiting can also be used as a means of indirectly "getting back at" at those who we feel are exploiting us. If you, or your partner, are constantly late for mutually agreed rendezvous, then you should confront the matter and try to pin down what is really being said.

Brian and Paul had an arrangement that Brian would buy the groceries for the week and on Friday Paul would pay him half the cost of the food they'd eaten. However, Paul always needed to be reminded about this arrangement and Brian began to feel bad about having to ask for the money every time. "At first I put it down to simple forgetfulness, but after a year I got suspicious. I felt as though I was asking for a hand-out instead of abiding by the arrangement we had made," he said. The barely concealed humiliation which Brian felt in having to ask for the money every time indicates clearly the aggression in Paul's "forgetfulness".

To deal with passive aggressive behaviour in your partner, it is as well to start off honestly and point out what you think is happening. Try to get to the source of the behaviour - what resentment is prompting him to act in this way? What is it about your relationship that is causing him to make this protest?

In other areas of life, passive aggressors need to be dealt with firmly to avoid the inconvenience they can cause. The chronic "misunderstander", for instance can be asked to repeat what you have agreed before they set about the task. In that way they cannot claim to have "misunderstood".

For the latecomer, a deadline needs to be set: "I'll met you at seven, and if you're not there by ten past, I'll be leaving."

2. Intellectualising

People who try to explain everything, try to rationalise feelings, can be hidden aggressors. Instead of simply accepting that feelings exist and are real to the person experiencing them, the intellectualiser tries to find the "reason" why. This often prevents the feelings being expressed and accepted and if they are negative feelings, it can mean that they become internalised and may show themselves in destructive behaviour.

3. The non-rewarder

When there is a power imbalance in a relationship, the person who may be dependent on his partner for reassurance can be kept in line by the non-rewarding of his achievements. He will never hear his partner say: "That was excellent" or "Well, done, I'm proud of you". Instead, anything he achieves is greeted with silence. When the person you most want to please appears indifferent, it makes you wonder whether it was any kind of achievement at all. In fact, the non-rewarder is actually using this aloofness as a method of control. By creating uncertainty he keeps his partner in line.

You can challenge a non-rewarder by asking: "What do you think of how I did?"

4. Doubting Thomases

These are the passive aggressors who like to throw cold water on your plans or who plant doubts in your mind when you are at your most vulnerable. Here's a Doubting Thomas in action, about to undermine his partner's efforts at improving his life:

"I think it would help me if I came out to my sister. She's always asking about you and I'm sure she knows we're having a relationship. I think I'll tell her the truth. It would be nice to have her as a friend again. I used to be so close to her, but we've drifted apart since I've been trying to keep my gayness from her."

Doubting Thomas replies: "I wouldn't if I were you. I thought I heard her making anti-gay remarks once. If you tell her she might react badly and tell you she never wants to see you again."

People who cast doubt on your plans and aspirations are usually trying to keep you in line. They are trying to stop you growing because they fear change themselves. The only way to defuse a Doubting Thomas is to directly challenge the throwing-cold-water-over-it technique. Point out the negativity and try to engage the person in a discussion of his real fears.

Leaving Manipulation Behind

Given the outside pressures, gay relationships need much effort to sustain. It is important that we also try to recognise and confront those pressures that are arising within. If you are honest with each other and accepting of each other's feelings, then there should be little temptation to use manipulative techniques to get your own way. This leaves you with more strength to face the hostile world together, united. Introducing assertiveness into your relationship will make you a stronger couple as well as stronger individuals.

9: ASSERTIVENESS AND SEX

There is little doubt that a successful sexual encounter can have an amazingly positive effect upon our self-esteem. When we have sex we become vulnerable because we are exposing to others some of our most fragile emotions. Each time we make love to someone we don't know very well, we take a calculated risk with our self-esteem. We take that risk because the need to make love is so strong. During love-making we have to let our partner see us with our guard down, and we have to trust him not to take a verbal pick-axe to our oh-so delicate sense of sexual confidence.

Needless to say, when sex goes wrong, our self-esteem can come crashing down like a falling factory chimney.

Failure And Fear of Failure

Two of the most common sexual difficulties experienced by men in the Western world are erection failure and premature ejaculation. When some men experience these problems they immediately begin to panic; they assume that there is something terribly wrong with them because they are not functioning perfectly at all times. Like most men in our society, they have probably been raised in an atmosphere of desperate machismo, where it is anathema to be anything less than a 'stud' - always ready, always willing, always able. The bragging and teasing about sexual performance which goes on between men creates a situation where no-one would dare admit that things might not always be perfect in the bedroom. Once such men have experienced an embarrassing episode of erection failure, they may become apprehensive about the next sexual encounter - what if they can't get it up again? One failure might be understandable, but twice? Without his erection he feels he is no longer a whole man and the anxiety which such self-imposed pressure can generate may lead to another bout of impotence. At this point the man is on a slippery slope. The vicious circle of fear is established - fear of failure and the fulfilment of that fear. He becomes deeply ashamed and afraid that other people will find out. To such a man no humiliation could be more dreaded than the prospect of his peers discovering that the only thing he can raise is a laugh. No humiliation could be more complete than having a lover point out the failings in his masculinity. So much self-esteem is invested in this impossible image of continuously perfect sexual functioning, that any crack in it can become a sense of failure as a whole human being.

The sex researchers Masters and Johnson investigated sexual dysfunction among homosexual men in their study *Homosexuality in Perspective* (Little, Brown, 1979). They discovered that impotence in gay men was more common than they had suspected and that some men who had become impotent were expert sexual "fakers" - finding ways of having sex without their partners suspecting that they were incapable of getting an erection. Masters and Johnson wrote:

> "It is far easier for homosexual men than for
> heterosexual men to succeed as sexual
> fakers...sexual fakery may be far more widespread
> among the male homosexual population than

previously suspected. The impotent homosexual male has at his disposal a most effective method of sexual fakery. He can easily assume a passive rather than an active role during sexual encounter. Once erective insecurity achieves dominance, the homosexual man tends to live a casual lifestyle, avoiding or dissolving committed relationships. If the impotent homosexual decides to pursue the path of sexual fakery, continuing relationships are quite threatening for they place the dysfunctional male in jeopardy. In a committed homosexual relationship, just as in a marriage, erective insecurity is virtually impossible to hide."

Masters and Johnson say that fear of the problem being publicly revealed often surfaces after there has been an episode of erection failure.

Typically, a gay man who is impotent, but who wants to have sex, will claim to his partners that he has little or no sexual drive of his own or that his sexual pleasure is mainly derived from stimulating and relieving his partner.

If all this sham fails to hide the problem, men with erection difficulties will frequently opt for the ultimate solution: withdrawing entirely from sexual life, and sometimes from social life, too. If the pattern of impotence begins at an early age, then the men involved can become reclusive. They live without relationships and often stay at home with ageing parents, confining themselves to family events and a few old friends. They may lose themselves in their careers or in their hobbies, such is their fear of being ridiculed or pitied because of their impotence.

One of the things all this tells us is that sexual ignorance is deeply ingrained in our society - if it weren't, so many men wouldn't imagine that their sex life was ended after one or two erection failures. They would know that all men have such experiences at some time in their life, and they wouldn't panic. In the vast majority of cases, erection failure and premature ejaculation are self-correcting, if properly understood and tackled sympathetically. (There are, of course, sometimes physical explanations for impotence, such as some medical conditions or the taking of certain medications.)

The second thing it tells us is that our mind has a huge effect on the workings of our body. Most incidents of erection failure are connected with stress, temporary illness, relationship difficulties, alcohol and drug abuse. Bad experiences in the past can also snowball into a severe problem with impotence that goes on for years, or even a lifetime.

For gay men there is another factor at work in instances of erection failure: the hatred of their sexuality. If you are consumed with guilt and shame about your homosexual feelings, then it is unlikely that you will get much pleasure from their expression. The anxiety and depression that is generated by your internalised homophobia will interfere with the functioning of your libido. Some gay men hate themselves so much that they never express their feelings for other men in a sexual way. They escape the feelings of shame in a number of ways: sometimes they enter the priesthood or a monastery. This takes from them the decision about whether to have sexual relationships. They hope to be relieved of the guilt of wanting to love other men.

However, the number of priests who fall by the wayside is enormous. The denial of their deepest desires can lead them into murky waters, and there have been several cases of priests abusing children in their care. Indeed, so worried is the Catholic Church about the rising number of priests who are failing to abide by their vows of celibacy, that they have set up a commission to look into the whole question.

Other gay men, who feel no calling to the religious life, will also opt for celibacy. They will invent elaborate rationales about why they cannot explore their sexuality ("My work is so demanding that I have no time for relationships" is a favourite) and they will discard any opportunity for real intimacy.

I have no desire to take away anyone's right to decide on the direction of their lives and, of course, celibacy can sometimes be a creative choice - for instance immediately after one partner dies, the other might want a period of sexual abstinence. I sometimes wonder, though, just how much of a choice most permanently celibate people have made. Perhaps the full acceptance and integration of their homosexuality into their lives isn't an option they've seriously considered. The prospect of that route is just too fearful for them.

And so, low gay self-esteem can interfere with the attainment of a satisfactory sex life, and it manifests itself in many ways, not only in the failure of erections, but in the very way we perceive sex and our sexual partners.

It follows from this that an increase in gay self-esteem will be an essential element in the attainment of a more satisfying sex life. If we don't like ourselves, it is unlikely that others will care much for us either. Assertiveness can help us not only get the kind of sex we want, it can also help us interact better and more sensitively with our partners.

Assertiveness can ensure that we introduce a kinder face to our sexual interactions, while at the same time ensuring that we do not allow ourselves to become involved in activities which we don't want or in relationships that are exploitative and unbalanced.

Safer sex, too, functions better when those practising it respect both themselves and those they are making love with.

205

The Safer Sex Problem

Statistics from clinics treating venereal diseases indicate that the incidence of HIV infection among gay men in Britain is once again on the increase. This is particularly true among those under twenty-five.

What are we to make of these figures? Why, after a period of slow decline in the gay community, has HIV infection begun to rise again? One factor - and I am sure there are many - could be that gay men are simply tired of following safer sex regimes which they consider to be boring and a hassle. It could be that they don't know about safer sex - although it's difficult to believe that after a decade of titanic effort by AIDS educators, the message hasn't got through to the majority. It may be that younger people never got the message in the first place. (This is possible, considering the reluctance of the educational establishment to include information about homosexuality and safer sex in the school curriculum.) It is also thought that many people under twenty-five are unwilling to believe that HIV is a problem for them. Youngsters naturally resist thinking about their own mortality - death is not an issue which concerns them. Several surveys have also shown that they consider HIV infection and AIDS to be "only a problem for the older generation". They reason that if they stick with people their own age for sex, they'll be safe.

Another explanation for this sudden upsurge in HIV infection might be that the low sexual self-esteem of many gay men can undermine their commitment to safer sex. They simply don't respect or value themselves enough to feel it matters. We have already seen the depth of loathing that some gay people feel about their sexuality; we have seen that it can cause them to act in a number of destructive ways - even, at some extremes, pushing them to suicide. This is why it is so important for gay people to work on their self-esteem. A keen sense of self-value - including valuing sexual orientation - is a major weapon in the fight against AIDS. People who love themselves, don't take potentially deadly risks.

Sex is easy to find in gay circles. The freewheeling days of the sixties and seventies may be gone, but there is still a strong feeling in the male gay community that sex is there to be enjoyed and not to be rationed. Young gay people are not willing to deny themselves the pleasures that their heterosexual counterparts take for granted. But just because sex is desired (and it is a pressing desire for most under-25s) and is easily available, doesn't mean that everyone knows how to cope with the complex human interactions that go with it. If you begin your sexual life with a low sense of self-esteem, vaguely ashamed of what you are doing, but still doing it because your body tells you to, then there are likely to be problems.

Young gay men who are anxious to explore their sexuality can come on to the gay scene to find themselves suddenly presented with myriad opportunities. They appear sophisticated, but underneath the bravado, they may be a mass of confusion, bewilderment and ignorance. They may not have the social skills that allow them to keep control of their own choices. They may want to say no to some propositions, but not know how. They may want to take precautions, but be afraid to ask for safer sex in case they are thought foolish or insulting. They may be under pressure from their peer group to do things that they would not otherwise choose to do.

This is not weakness, it is simply inexperience. Judging by the way we deprive our children of information about sex and human relationships, you'd imagine that society considers ignorance to be bliss. It is not. A dearth of knowledge on sexual and emotional matters can lead to many problems later in life. This is particularly true of young gay people, who are unlikely to receive any practical information from either home or school.

Those starting out on their first sexual explorations in the gay world need not be particularly young, though. We spoke earlier of the stages of "coming out" that gay people experience, and that sometimes the process can take as long as fifteen years. As a consequence of this "developmental lag", some gay people don't have their first sexual experience until well into their twenties - or even later. They must wait until this time for what most heterosexuals experience in adolescence.

It can then take a lot of exploration and experimentation before gay people know precisely what it is they want from their emotional and sexual lives. In the meantime, the danger of having unprotected sex is always there.

Taking Control Of Our Sexual Selves

Let's think back to the Four Golden Rules of Assertiveness and try to apply them to our sexual lives. When we meet someone new, who we find attractive and with whom we'd like to have sex, the same principles still apply: your feelings and needs are sacrosanct, they are as important as anyone else's and it is your duty to protect them - without trampling over those of others; you are not responsible for the way others feel and they are not responsible for the way you feel; you don't have to explain your feelings. In this context there is another rule: you should make every effort to protect your health and safety.

So let's follow Shane, who's twenty-one and about to embark on his first date.

Shane has had problems coming to terms with his sexuality. It has taken him a long time to be able to admit to himself that he's gay. His years of resistance to the truth have made him into a nervous, shy sort of person. He still lives at home with his aged father, but he hasn't come out. Shane's only sexual experience to date happened by accident when he was taken short while driving in the country. He noticed a public lavatory on the side of the road and stopped for a pee. When he got inside the convenience, there was another man standing at the urinal. As Shane took his leak, he noticed that the man was looking over the urinal and down at his penis. Shane had heard about men frequenting public lavatories for sex, but he'd never seen anyone doing it - until now. He had imagined that dirty old men did this kind of thing, and he'd been quite sickened by the idea. But this man wasn't old. He was a business man in a conventional suit and tie.

Although he had made a pact with himself that he would never have sex with another man, because he thought it was perverted, Shane paused at the urinal long after he had finished urinating. He looked over at the man who was openly masturbating. Shane knew that this was an opportunity that he probably wouldn't have again - he normally avoided public lavatories because they were dirty and smelly - and he had to make a decision. The feelings that he had been repressing came flooding back to him, and he found himself excited by the prospect of sex. The man smiled, Shane smiled back and the man took this as a signal to reach over and fondle Shane.

Shane was worried that someone might come wandering in, so the man signalled that they should go into a lavatory stall. Once inside, Shane masturbated the man. The man tried to return the favour, but Shane was unable to rise to the occasion.

It was over in a couple of minutes, and both men hurried furtively from the lavatory and back to their cars. They had not spoken, or even looked each other in the eyes.

Shane was overwhelmed with guilt. He felt dirty and was disgusted with himself for having done such a thing. From that moment on he decided that he would never again have sex with a man.

And yet, over the following weeks the incident haunted his mind. Yes, it had been a guilt-ridden experience for him, but it had also been strangely reassuring and exciting. Surely there was something better, somewhere? All the same, he used the encounter as masturbation fantasy. When he was on his own, he had no problems with erections.

He decided that he would have to do something about these feelings that were now becoming obsessive.

What Shane Did

Now Shane is at the local gay group for the first time and has met William, who is twenty-eight. They were both attracted to each other immediately. Shane will be the first to admit that he went to the group in the hope that he would meet someone to have sex with. He has been fantasising about finding a good-looking man and now his dream has come true. William is tall, dark-haired, works out regularly, and has a gorgeous smile. He also has a flat of his own, and invites Shane round after the meeting for coffee.

When they get to the flat, Shane realises that William is far more experienced than he is. There are gay magazines laying around and on the telephone answering machine are intimate messages, one from a man named John and the other from someone called Nick. Shane begins to get a little nervous - this is the first time he's had such a deliberately-planned sexual encounter and he's not sure he'll know what to do.

Instead of coffee, William produces a bottle of gin. He pours one for Shane, who takes it because he feels it would look silly if he doesn't. He hasn't drunk anything stronger than cider up until now. He hates the taste of the gin, it makes him want to vomit, but he forces it down, trying to hide his nauseous feelings.

William sits beside him, and after a couple more drinks he says: "Do you fancy going to bed?" Shane nods enthusiastically. At last the dream is going to come true, and with someone as handsome as William. He can hardly believe it. This doesn't have the sordid associations that the cottage encounter did. William is not ashamed of himself, and is honest and relaxed about what he wants. His flat is clean, nicely decorated and the bedroom is romantically lit.

William undresses. He has a beautiful body, and Shane is a little self-conscious about his own puny frame. But he quickly undresses, too, and slips between the sheets. William gets in with him, and they are soon kissing and cuddling and rubbing their bodies together. William's hands are wandering, and Shane feels as though he is in paradise. He loves the firmness of William's body, the hotness of his breath on his neck, the hairiness of his legs, the strength of his arms. This is how he had imagined sex would be.

He decides just to let it all happen - and the gin has certainly helped lower his inhibitions.

William's hands are now between Shane's legs, and his fingers are prodding at his arse, which is pleasant at first. But as William becomes rougher with his fingers, Shane begins to feel pain. He doesn't really know whether it's supposed to be like this, so he doesn't protest. William seems to be enjoying himself, and that's the main thing.

Shane has long hoped for the opportunity to suck a man off, and as this seems to be dreams-come-true time, he slips down the bed in the hope that William will enjoy his oral attentions. But William pushes him away: "I don't like sucking," he says. Shane is disappointed, but says nothing.

After a while, William stops the rough handling of Shane's rear end, much to Shane's relief, but then he whispers: "Can I fuck you, Shane?"

Shane is well aware of what is being asked of him. He has fantasised often enough what it would be like to have a man make love to him in this way. He is apprehensive, but says yes. Shane reaches over for a tube of K-Y, and applies some of the jelly to himself. Then he turns Shane over and tries to push his penis in. Shane feels a sudden surge of agonising pain, so intense that he actually sees stars. William begins thrusting, and with each push the pain surges through him again. He cannot help but grimace and whimper. He is trying not to scream because he knows that other people do this and apparently enjoy it. He doesn't want to seem stupid or inexperienced, but he had not imagined that it would be so unpleasant.

After what seems like hours, William eventually reaches orgasm, while still inside Shane. He then collapses in a heap of exhaustion. He rolls over, panting, and almost immediately falls asleep. Shane lays there feeling let down. He has had no pleasure at all from the encounter, only pain.

Shane's guts feel as though they are on fire. He climbs out of bed and goes to the bathroom feeling sick and unhappy. As he sits there he remembers what he has read about safer sex, how it is dangerous not to use a condom when having anal intercourse. In all the excitement, he hadn't thought about it, and William hadn't mentioned it either. Now he begins to feel a little bit frightened. What has he done? Could he have become infected with HIV? Surely not by William, he is so healthy-looking, in fact he is the picture of vitality with his glowing skin and sculpted chest. He decides that there is nothing to worry about - except that William didn't seem to care about anything but his own enjoyment. Although, in some ways, Shane had enjoyed being made love to - the strange feeling of power that he experienced through giving William so much pleasure - Shane is still feeling extremely fruity, but William is asleep.

He climbs back into the bed and tries to sleep beside William, but he can't. He is too upset about what has happened. Surely he too is entitled to some kind of satisfaction?

He lays there through the night, not wanting to turn over in case he wakes William, feeling pins and needles in his legs and letting his arm get numb before carefully rolling on to his back.

The following morning, William wakes at about six-thirty. He puts his arm over Shane, who is tense and tired. William is feeling sexy again. "Do you want to do it again?" William asks.

Shane finds himself saying "yes" in the hope that this time it will be different, and once more William is reaching for the K-Y. Shane thinks that he should say something about condoms, but he hesitates because if he mentions them William might be insulted. Would he imagine that Shane was suggesting he had AIDS? Would he be angry and cause a scene? Would even the limited pleasure of another one-sided love-making session be denied?

Ten minutes later, it is all over and William is under the shower. It has been an almost exact replay of the previous night, except that when he had finished, William had gone to the bathroom instead of falling asleep. He seemed totally unaware that Shane might need some stimulation, too.

Shane is even more frustrated and annoyed, but he says nothing because - well, he is in William's house, and he didn't know him very well, and he didn't want to upset him.

Eventually, when he realises that William is getting dressed and that their encounter is over, Shane gets out of bed and puts his own clothes on.

"Want a cup of coffee?" William asks as he plugs in the percolator. Shane sits at the table, and is once more enchanted by how handsome William looks. They have breakfast together.

"Is everything OK?" William asks.

"Oh yes, fine," says Shane.

"Good. Well, I'm afraid I've got to go to work now, but thanks for a great evening."

Shane is out on the street now, watching William drive away to his job. There has been no mention of exchanging telephone numbers or seeing each other again, and Shane didn't have the courage to suggest it. Perhaps William was just being polite and didn't really like him very much. He couldn't face the prospect of suggesting another meeting in case William said no. The rejection would have been more than he could bear.

Shane goes home feeling strange about the whole experience, but not knowing why it didn't worked out.

In this little scenario, Shane's first proper sexual encounter (discounting the cottage) has proved extremely disappointing, and has also put Shane at risk. But Shane didn't have the confidence or the skills to put these things right. We have to make some allowances for his inexperience. He has had little opportunity to find out what is expected of him in situations like this. He doesn't yet have the confidence to ask for what he wants or to insist on safer sex. But these are skills he must quickly master if he is to have a better and safer time.

Now Shane is twenty-three and has learned a lot about sexual etiquette. He has learned what he likes and what he doesn't like, and how to ask for it. He has also found out how to discover what other people like, and tries to ensure that both parties enjoy the encounter. But, above all, he has educated himself about safer sex. What he found out frightened him. His unsafe adventure began to play on his mind and a few months after his experience with William, he decided that he would test for HIV. He went along to his local special clinic and had the test done. There was a week to wait for the result. It was the longest week he had ever spent. He didn't sleep properly, wasn't interested in his food and was extremely anxious. He tried to imagine what he would do if the test proved positive, and many unpleasant thoughts went through his mind. The worst part of all was that he couldn't share his fears with anyone, especially not his father who would be horrified.

Shane was lucky, the test proved negative, but the trauma of taking it shook him profoundly, and he made a pact with himself that from then on, safer sex was the only option.

With the benefit of his experience, let's follow Shane into his latest sexual episode:

The pub is full this particular Saturday night and there is a heavy, cruisy atmosphere. The music is throbbing loudly and the air is smoky. Across the room is a tall, thick-set man wearing a leather jacket. Shane noticed him the moment he walked into the bar. They have exchanged glances, and Shane has gained the impression that the man might be interested, so he slowly works his way over to where he is standing and offers to buy him a drink. By the end of the evening, they have arrived at Shane's place, a modest terraced house which he has recently moved into.

The man is called Dave. Despite his threatening appearance (with his swarthy, moustachioed face and heavy, leather clothes) he is a friendly guy with a ready smile.

They are soon undressed and passionately snogging on the settee.

"What do you like to do?" Dave asks after a while.

"I'd really like to suck you," says Shane. Dave is happy to oblige.

They make their way to the bedroom, and Shane asks Dave what his preference is. Dave is really anxious to make love to Shane anally.

"I'd love to," says Shane, "but I'm afraid I don't do that. I only do safer sex..."

"Well, so do I," says Dave, "I've got some johnnys in my coat pocket."

"I'm sorry, I don't want to have anal sex at all."

Dave seems a little miffed by Shane's reluctance, and tries cajoling him. "Oh, come on. It's safe with a condom. You've got me really hot and now you're backing off."

"I'm not backing off," Shane says with a lascivious grin, "I'm as hot as you are." He puts his mouth next to Dave's ear and whispers "I don't mind if you fuck me between the cheeks of my arse. In fact, I'd love you to."

Dave smiles and needs no further persuasion to try this and finds it most pleasurable. Later they try numerous other non-penetrative variations, including 69-ing, body rubbing, licking and Shane gets out his box of sex toys for them to play with. By dawn they decide that they really ought to try and get some sleep. Both are content, and happy with their encounter.

The assertiveness skills that Shane is now putting into practice have been gained the hard way. He has learned from the disasters of his earlier attempts at sexual pleasure. He knows how to ask for what he wants, to say what he doesn't want and to negotiate safer sex effectively. Because he treated Dave as an equal with equally important feelings, they were able to function better in bed together. Both knew exactly where they stood with each other.

But honest speaking in sexual situations is not always easy. We have said how fragile some men's sense of their sexuality is, and how easily it can be destroyed by bad experiences. It is because of this fragility that we have to be particularly sensitive in using assertiveness in our most intimate moments. It is when we are in bed with our partner that we have to carefully screen out any brutality which might be posing as honesty. We must respect our partner's feelings and accept their validity.

What we don't want is an irresistible force meeting an immovable object so that the result is tenseness and conflict. Aggressiveness might be OK for some aspects of sex, but not in the negotiating process.

The things that might stand in the way of successfully negotiating safer sex are:

1. **Not knowing how to talk about sex.** *Many people know how to* do *sex, but not how to* talk *about it. They may have been raised in a family that was reluctant to discuss sexual matters (the majority of families fall into this category), and subsequently they become embarrassed when they have to put their feelings into words - especially their feelings about sex.*

Why not spend some time practising the art of talking about sex? Can you persuade a friend to help you out with this? There are different kinds of sexual language that people use: the medical and scientific, the literary and the slang. Find out what kind of sexual language you are most comfortable with. Try saying the words out loud. Are you going to say "cock" or "penis"? "Masturbate" or "wank"? "Fuck" or "make love"? Whichever version trips easiest from your tongue and causes least cringing is the one to use with your lover.

Even if you keep it to the absolute minimum, you should still have a vocabulary that you can use without hesitation. And the more you use the words, the more familiar they become and the less difficult they are to say.

Your partner might also have problems in vocalising preferences or desires and may be relieved if you take the lead and allow direct talking without embarrassment.

2. **Not wanting to insult your partner.** *Just like Shane, we might be worried that if we suggest safer sex, our partner is going to take umbrage. We don't want to give the impression that we think they're anything other than wonderful, and as soon as condoms are suggested, there is the inference that the person might have AIDS or be HIV positive.*

You should stop seeing it from this point of view. Taking precautions which might save your life is no reason to be insulted. Your partner should be grateful - after all, you're suggesting safer sex as much for his protection as for yours.

If you do get an "I'm insulted" response from a partner when you suggest safer sex, you should remember the skills of assertiveness and tell him clearly and directly that what you are suggesting is not an intended insult, but is common sense. Don't apologise for trying to protect yourself - and him.

Those who say they are "hurt" by your inference that they may be infected with HIV, and expect you to drop the subject because of their feelings, need to be challenged. If you avoid negotiating safer sex because of fears of "hurt feelings" then you are, in effect, depriving your partner of the opportunity to learn a valuable lesson. Hurt feelings can be repaired, but HIV infection cannot.

3. **Not wanting to risk spoiling an opportunity for sex.** *It could be that you've just met the man of your dreams and you're absolutely determined that you're going to have sex with him. You are anxious not to miss this opportunity, so you are unwilling to do anything that might spoil your chances. He doesn't mention safer sex, so you don't.*

This is a difficult one, because the impetus for sex can be extremely strong, and the desire not to put an opportunity at risk can overrule all good intentions. But keep it in proportion. If you're going to take foolish risks with *this* individual, you might be prepared to do it with others. Becoming HIV positive and maybe getting AIDS is not going to give you a long and sexy life. One unsafe sexual episode can be all it takes to acquire HIV, so there can be no exceptions in a safer sex regime. A commitment to safer sex is a commitment to your own long-term survival. And besides, your irresistible hunk might just be waiting for you to make the first suggestion about safer sex! He might also need to be educated. You can show him how to have sex safely - and everyone will be happy.

4. **Not really knowing what safer sex is.** *Younger gay people (the very young) might be excused for not knowing the ins and outs of safer sex, but the majority of gay people can't convincingly claim such ignorance.*

There has been a huge education campaign stretching over many years directed at gay men, and you won't be around on the gay scene for very long before you hear all about it. Condoms are available freely and easily in all kinds of places. If you aren't sure about the details of what's safe and what isn't, contact one of the agencies that deal with HIV and

AIDS prevention (such as The Terrence Higgins Trust) and ask for some information.

5. **Being under the influence of alcohol or drugs.** *Gay socialising often entails the drinking of large amounts of alcohol; drugs may also be readily available. These are mind-altering substances, and can cause us to behave in ways that we wouldn't dream of doing when sober.*

The answer is to make as many preparations as possible before you set out when your mind is clear. Make sure there are condoms available wherever you might need them (keep some in your pocket, some in your bedside table, some in the kitchen, in your car or any other area where you are likely to have sex). If you're out with friends, ask them to remind you to "play safely" if you are going off with someone you've met during the evening. Try to get yourself into a mindset that says however drunk you are, you're not going to take stupid risks.

If it looks as though you're going to have sex, start the negotiation about safe alternatives at an early stage. Don't wait until you've got your clothes off and are at the height of passion, when stopping becomes much more difficult. An assertive way to negotiate safer sex might go something like this:

"I'd love to have sex with you, but I always make it a rule to practise safer sex."

"Why, do you think I'm going to give you something, or what?"

"No, I don't think you're going to give me something. I just make it a rule for myself only to do safer sex."

"Oh this safe sex rubbish is only for people who screw around with older men. I'm only nineteen and you're only twenty. We ain't got AIDS".

"All the same, I'd rather stick to my rule. Is that OK?"

You can then either say what you'd like to do, or simply let it happen with both of you knowing the boundaries you've set. It might even be possible to arrange a little signal that you can use if you feel that things are going too close to being unsafe - a slap on the bottom, perhaps or a tug of the hair. A small, unspoken signal like that can convey a message without taking the heat out of the moment.

Those With HIV Infection Or Aids

Some people who are living with HIV infection and AIDS will become so nervous about the implications of their condition that they will stop having sex altogether. Although they may still want the comfort and intimacy that sex gives, they may feel guilty and confused about what they should tell potential partners. What is the right thing to do if you are HIV-positive, free of symptoms, looking well, and a sexual opportunity presents itself? Is it your duty to tell the other person of your status or should you simply insist on safer sex and say nothing?

There can be no hard and fast rule about this. In the end it is a personal decision, and many gay men have wrestled with it. Not only do they want to ensure that they don't infect anyone else, they are also anxious that they do not become pariahs and outcasts. They may want sex and closeness with other human beings more than ever because of their understandable feelings of insecurity.

The tabloid press tells lurid tales of those with HIV who 'deliberately' set out to infect others as a perverse sort of revenge. Although there may be some people like that, I think they are rare. Most men who have HIV infection will be concerned that no-one else gets it from them. But safer sex is a two-way proposition, it is necessary for both partners to take responsibility. No-one can infect you with HIV during consenting sex unless you permit it. It is as much your responsibility to prevent infected semen getting into your body as it is the other person's. A commitment to safer sex is the only answer.

There are advertisements in the personal columns of the gay press in which people who are HIV positive advertise for others in the same situation in order to make relationships. This seems, on the surface, like a good idea, but it is not entirely without complications. Two people who are HIV positive would be unwise to simply say: "What have we to lose? We can forget safer sex." There is more than one strain of HIV, and through unsafe sex, it is possible for another variety to be acquired. It is also possible that other harmful viruses and bacteria might be passed on, further compromising the immune system.

When those with HIV reveal their status to potential new partners, they may face painful rejection. They will have taken an emotional battering with the diagnosis itself; the last thing their ego needs is repeated rebuffs from would-be lovers. As long as they don't put their partners at risk, they may feel it justifiable to avoid the trauma of rejection by omitting mention of their health status.

An article in *The Sunday Express* (17th January, 1993) looked at the problems of those with HIV finding partners. The article included an interview with 46-year-old interior designer Don Benschneider, who was diagnosed as HIV positive seven years ago. Don had decided to place a personal ad in the hope of finding a lover. "I didn't want to face another year, possibly my last, without a partner," he said. He composed his ad in such a way that it eliminated those who were newly-diagnosed and those who were in the last stages of the disease. He didn't have the energy either to support those who were going through the crisis of adjustment that recent diagnosis brings, nor to make a commitment to someone who would soon die. Don says the ad achieved its goal. "I think I have found the right partner," he says. "Everyone with HIV should try this."

Another interviewee was Geoff, who was diagnosed as positive in 1988. He placed an ad in the lifestyle magazine *Sky*. "I said I was HIV positive, healthy with a young attitude and loveable looks, looking for love and sex." He said he received two replies, neither of them from HIV positive men. He decided not to follow them up, as he had wanted someone who was in the same situation as he was. He says: "My closest friend is the only person I've told, I keep it to myself because of the ignorance of other people who wouldn't understand. And there's the sympathy, I couldn't handle that. At the moment I'm treated normally, which is how I like it."

The article also described the experiences of Peter, who was diagnosed in 1987. He says he placed the ad as a last resort. Although he described himself as "straight-acting, attractive, HIV positive, happy and looking for an uncomplicated man" he was, in reality, "feeling very low". His relationship with his boyfriend Alan had ended after his diagnosis. "I felt lost. I have a close circle of friends and family who know, but I felt alone...I find the gay scene intimidating, so that door was closed to me. Besides, if I were to go out and meet someone - telling them you're HIV positive is very stressful. And once you've told them, you might not see them for dust."

Although Peter didn't receive any replies to his ad, Alan has now returned to him and they are having another go at their relationship.

Keeping self-esteem high in this situation is difficult. Seek out others who are in a similar situation, and take advantage of the powerful networks of support that have been created for those with HIV infection and AIDS. And remember that in order to resist the insidious effects of the virus, a strong sense of self-respect will be needed. Find others who have been there before you and who have discovered methods of building that vital determination to survive. Learn from them.

One of the greatest methods of rebuilding damaged self-esteem for those with HIV infection is the adoption of a health maintenance regimen, and a commitment to long-term survival. There are several self-help books available for those who want to take charge of their own health after being diagnosed HIV-positive, and there are organisations which can give information about the various options which are available. Taking responsibility and actively pursuing a healthy lifestyle will give you a focus. You will need to take decisions and discipline yourself to make changes in diet, routine and ways of thinking. You may want to explore more deeply the philosophy of holistic treatments as well as keeping abreast of developments in conventional medicine. There may be stress-reduction techniques you can use, such as relaxation and visualisation. All these methods are worth consideration and, when you take your health seriously and make a commitment to ensuring that you stay well, you will find that a wonderful thing happens to your self-esteem and your confidence. It will begin to grow again, and you will realise that you are valuing yourself at the most basic level - protecting and nurturing your very life. There can be nothing more beneficial to self-esteem than that.

Long Term Sexual Relationships

Participants in long term sexual relationships do not necessarily conduct themselves assertively. Sometimes couples who have been together for years have no more success in communicating properly than those who have only recently met. Experience does not necessarily make things easier and, indeed, some couples plod along accepting that their sex lives are unsatisfactory without really knowing what they can do to change things.

If your relationship is unsatisfactory, it is going to take a commitment from both partners to change. Many of the suggestions about assertiveness and communication can be applied to long-term relationships, as long as both partners agree. However, if a destructive pattern of arguing and aggression has become established, it needs to be challenged and replaced. Those couples who value their relationships and want them to function better will be willing to sit down together and honestly examine their behaviour. Some may need the objective view of an outsider and would benefit from counselling.

Those in long-term relationships may have already worked out their own compromises about sex. If sexual activity between the two partners has diminished, or even ceased, the partners might want to negotiate alternatives. Many gay couples - statistics would say most of them - accept that one or both partners will have sex outside the primary relationship. So long as this is acceptable to both parties, and that only safer sex is practised, it can be a way forward.

It is unrealistic to expect the same level of sexual activity that is common at the beginning of a relationship to continue over many years, and assertiveness can help in the negotiation of compromises and alternatives. It might be useful to discuss early in the relationship attitudes to monogamy, bearing in mind that over a long period people's attitudes can change.

Other couples find that their sexual interest in each other continues over the years and they have no desire for other partners. But they still need to practise their assertiveness and communication skills to ensure that complacency doesn't breed contempt. Here are a few tips that long-term partners can apply in their efforts at sexual communication:

1. Try to accentuate to positive in negotiating sex. Don't say "you never..." say "I'd love it if you..."

2. Join together to tackle problems. Don't say "What are you going to do about it?" say "What are we going to do about it?"

3. Don't allow partners' "hurt feelings" to stop you from saying what must be said. So long as it is not expressed with the intention of hurting, it is better to be straightforward about problems than avoid them.

4. Don't be put off from asking for changes because you are afraid your partner will be "upset". Constantly rescuing partners from their own mistakes in this way does not allow them to learn, and it also compromises your own needs and feelings.

5. Some people don't know how to ask for intimacy without sex. Sometimes non-sexual closeness can be all that is desired, and it pays to know how to recognise when you feel like that. Sex is not mandatory. Accept that it doesn't have to go 'all the way' every time. Quickies can be fun!

6. Occasional conflict is both an unavoidable and essential part of any relationship. The secret is to try and use the conflict constructively.

Relationships can become more dignified if freed from the burden of constant and pointless bickering. The aim is to establish new and better means of communicating.

10: MOVING ON

Assertiveness isn't simply a set of problem-solving tricks which you can apply when the going gets rough: it is a lifeskill. To make assertiveness work you not only have to learn the techniques but also revise the attitudes which have prevented you from being assertive before. This probably means challenging deeply held ideas about yourself and who you are; you will probably have to rethink convictions that you have, until now, taken for granted. It isn't easy to do this at the best of times, but is considerably harder when your confidence is low.

Facing up to your homosexuality after maybe years of either resenting it or avoiding it, also means taking risks. If you feel the life that you have at present could be made more fulfilling and less frustrating, then tackle the reorganisation with determination. After the almost inevitable setbacks will come the opportunity for growth and greater happiness.

We identified at the beginning of this book the stages of a gay person's "coming out". But getting through that process can be a long, challenging and painful business. It can take some men anything up to fifteen years, (a few even longer and, alas, others a lifetime) for people to reach the stage where their homosexuality is integrated as a legitimate element of their whole personality. It is at that stage that their homosexual orientation ceases to be a major issue and becomes a simple aspect of the complete person. I think we can assume that the American composer Ned Rorem had completed his own coming out journey when he wrote: "homosexuality, unlike negritude or womanhood, is a part-time job". And so it should be. But for those individuals who have failed to progress on their journey of self-discovery, homosexuality can become a fear-generating obsession. It is people who claim that their sexual orientation is "not important" (because they are trying to avoid it) who are likely to suffer most. By denying that homosexuality is an important issue which must be dealt with, people with low gay self-esteem are depriving themselves of the opportunity for a full and satisfying life.

Enlisting Help

The vast majority of people cope as best they can with the coming out journey. Few seek professional assistance. However, you might want to enlist the help of a therapist or counsellor who understands the issues. This can be an expensive business, but if you can afford it and feel that it would be useful to you, here are a few tips for finding a good therapist.

1. Make sure your counsellor or therapist is properly trained and qualified. The British Association of Counselling, 1 Regent Place, Rugby CV21 2PJ, will send a list of members in your area, which will also tell you about their qualifications.

There is also a gay counselling service called PACE (Project for Advice, Counselling & Education), 2 Shelburne Road, London N7 6DL Tel: 071-700 1323.

2. Don't commit yourself to a course of counselling or therapy until you are sure that the practitioner you have contacted is right for you. Remember, you are the customer and you have a right to shop around. Some therapists will offer a free initial consultation so that you can see how you get on, and assess how comfortable you feel with each other. Make sure you use this consultation to find out whether the therapist understands the specific issues that you want to explore. The training of straight counsellors now includes some of the topics which will be specific to their gay clients, and most have a sympathetic and informed approach. However, you may still feel that a gay or lesbian counsellor or therapist would be more helpful.

Be especially careful to ensure that anyone offering "gay counselling" is not approaching the issue from a religious point of view. There are several organisations run by fundamentalist Christians which offer what they call "counselling" which is in fact an attempt to "cure" gay people of their homosexual orientation. Such organisations create more problems than they solve and should be assiduously avoided by anyone seeking to become a happy homosexual.

Ensure, too, that you check anyone who advertises in the gay press thoroughly - remember, anyone can set up as a counsellor, and those who do so without proper training can often cause more problems than they solve as they draw out painful issues which they can't deal with. You should also be wary of people who have taken up counselling as a method of dealing with their own problems.

3. Ask these questions when either making the initial approach to a counsellor or at the initial consultation: What are your qualifications? How long have you been counselling? How will the sessions be organised? What method of working do you use?

If they hold a recognised qualification, and have been counselling for some years, then you can feel more secure that they know their stuff.

He or she will tell you what kind of therapist he or she is, and if you have never heard of the technique they use (Jungian, Reichian, hypnotherapy, transactional analysis) ask questions about it.

Also ask a few pertinent questions about his or her attitudes to homosexuality. If you detect any lack of understanding or even a trace of hostility, then maybe you'd be better off trying elsewhere. Many heterosexual therapists welcome gay clients because working together allows personal discovery and growth for the therapist, too.

If there is any reluctance to give you comprehensive information, then ask yourself why. If you feel uneasy about anything that has been said during your enquiry, take your time before making a decision. Think about it for a few days. Trust your instincts to tell you whether this is the right person for you.

4. Counsellors and therapists can charge what they like, but in 1993 the usual fee is about £25-£30 per session. If you feel that you may need a long period of consultation, then obviously it is likely prove very expensive. It is important, though, to stick with it, even during periods when you might feel angry with your counsellor (although a perpetual feeling of antipathy towards the practitioner might mean there is a more serious problem, and you might want to consider whether to leave). Don't feel that you are unable to terminate the treatment if you think it is upsetting you more than is necessary, but do bear in mind that if you are confronting difficult issues it won't always be plain sailing. In the end, you are the customer, and you have a right to behave assertively with your practitioner if you feel the situation calls for it.

Putting It All Together

Applying assertive behaviour to those areas of our life which make us anxious can have a dramatic effect on the way we see ourselves. Far from being powerless, we become powerful. We suddenly discover that it is possible to control the way our life progresses instead of feeling that we are at the mercy of other people's needs and feelings. Being an assertively gay person means, in the end, being a happier and healthier homosexual.

One gay man said that his coming out process had been "a journey without maps" - a hit and miss affair - and he had taken many painful wrong turnings along the road. But gradually the maps are being drawn for gay people and, although we are all, to some extent, masters of our own destiny, we can profit from the experiences of others and avoid the pitfalls that delayed them on their journeys. Assertiveness is not the whole answer, but it is a wonderful tool which can speed us on our way.

Bon Voyage!

Other Books by Terry Sanderson

MAKING GAY RELATIONSHIPS WORK
A handbook for Male Couples   **£4. 95 + 75p p&p**
The best-selling guide to making your relationship work. Includes chapters on: The Initial Meeting; Three Cornerstones of Successful Relationships; Negotiation; Sustaining Good Sex; Getting Your Relationship Out of the Closet - and much more.
"This is the book to keep under your pillow" - Pink Paper
"Probably the most sensible, useful and readable book you will find on your bookshelf at the moment" - Gay Community News

A STRANGER IN THE FAMILY
How To Cope If Your Child Is Gay   **£5. 95 + 75p p&p**
A practical and reassuring handbook for parents who have just discovered they have a gay child. Packed with advice on such topics as how to cope with the initial crisis; how parents handle their own 'coming out'; the religious dilemma; the significance of AIDS; coping with a gay child's friends and lovers. This unique book will help parents survive the crisis of their son or daughter's coming out and enable them to make better, more honest relationships.
"Wise, informed, compassionate and humane" - Dan O'Hara

HOW TO BE A HAPPY HOMOSEXUAL
The Gay Men's Handbook for the 1990s   **£4.95 + 75p p&p**
The new GMP edition of this seminal work contains practical information on topics as varied and relevant as coming out, forming relationships, enjoying safer sex, the law and coping with homophobia.
"This is a splendid book, honestly felt, honestly written, honestly presented" - Claire Rayner

**From bookshops or by post: The Other Way Press,
PO Box 130, London W5 1DQ**